WITHDRAWN FROM
KENT STATE UNIVERSITY LIBRARIES

AMERICAN FAMILIAR VERSE
VERS DE SOCIÉTÉ
BRANDER MATTHEWS

AMERICAN
FAMILIAR VERSE
VERS DE SOCIÉTÉ

EDITED, WITH AN INTRODUCTION
BY
BRANDER MATTHEWS, Litt.D. (Yale)
OF COLUMBIA UNIVERSITY

GRANGER POETRY LIBRARY

GRANGER BOOK CO., INC.
Great Neck, N.Y.

First Published 1904
Reprinted 1982

LC 81-84880
ISBN 0-89609-232-1

TO

MY FRIEND AND COLLEAGUE

FRANK DEMPSTER SHERMAN

JOCOSA LYRA

In our hearts is the Great One of Avon
  Engraven,
And we climb the cold summits once built on
  By Milton.
But at times not the air that is rarest
  Is fairest,
And we long in the valley to follow
  Apollo.
Then we drop from the heights atmospheric
  To Herrick,
Or we pour the Greek honey, grown blander,
  Of Landor;
Or our cosiest nook in the shade is
  Where Praed is,
Or we toss the light bells of the mocker
  With Locker.
Oh, the song where not one of the Graces
  Tight-laces —
Where we woo the sweet muses not starchly,
  But archly —
Where the verse, like the piper a-Maying,
  Comes playing —
And the rhyme is as gay as a dancer
  In answer —
It will last till men weary of pleasure
  In measure!
It will last till men weary of laughter . . .
  And after!

AUSTIN DOBSON.

CONTENTS

	Page
INTRODUCTION	1
BENJAMIN FRANKLIN. 1706–1790	
Paper	39
FRANCIS HOPKINSON. 1737–1791	
Song	41
ELIZABETH GRAEME FERGUSON. 1739–1801	
The Country Parson	42
NATHANIEL EVANS. 1742–1767	
An Ode (attempted in the manner of Horace) to my Ingenious Friend, Mr. Thomas Godfrey	43
PHILIP FRENEAU. 1752–1832	
The Parting Glass	45
On the Ruins of a Country Inn	47
To a Caty-Did	49
ROYALL TYLER. 1757–1826	
My Mistresses	51
The Bookworm	53
SAMUEL LOW. 1765–?	
To a Segar	55
JOHN QUINCY ADAMS. 1767–1848	
To Sally	56
WILLIAM MARTIN JOHNSON. 1771–1797	
On Snow-flakes melting on his Lady's Breast	58

CONTENTS

JOHN SHAW. 1778–1809   Page
   Song 59
CLEMENT CLARKE MOORE. 1779–1863
   A Visit from St. Nicholas 60
JAMES KIRKE PAULDING. 1779–1860
   The Old Man's Carousal 62
WASHINGTON IRVING. 1783–1859
   Album Verses 64
   A Certain Young Lady 66
WILLIAM MAXWELL. 1784–1857
   To a Fair Lady 68
   To Anne 69
WILLIAM CULLEN BRYANT. 1794–1878
   Robert of Lincoln 70
FITZGREENE HALLECK. 1790–1867
   Ode to Fortune 73
   Woman 75
JOSEPH RODMAN DRAKE. 1795–1820
   The Man Who Frets at Worldly Strife . . . 77
   Inconstancy 78
   To a Lady 79
EDWARD COATE PINKNEY. 1802–1828
   A Health 80
ALBERT GORTON GREENE. 1802–1868
   Old Grimes 82
RALPH WALDO EMERSON. 1803–1882
   The Humble-Bee 84
NATHANIEL PARKER WILLIS. 1806–1867
   Love in a Cottage 87
CHARLES FENNO HOFFMAN. 1806–1884
   Sparkling and Bright 89
   Rosalie Clare 90

CONTENTS

JOHN GREENLEAF WHITTIER. 1807–1892   Page
In School-Days 91
The Barefoot Boy 93
The Henchman 97

HENRY WADSWORTH LONGFELLOW. 1807–1882
Catawba Wine 99
A Dutch Picture 102
Beware 104

OLIVER WENDELL HOLMES. 1809–1894
Contentment 106
To an Insect 109
The Last Leaf 111
On Lending a Punch-Bowl 113
Bill and Joe 115
Dorothy Q 117

FRANCES SARGENT OSGOOD. 1811–1850
A Dancing Girl 120

JOHN GODFREY SAXE. 1816–1887
The Mourner à la Mode 121
The Heart and the Liver 123
Little Jerry, the Miller 125
My Familiar 127
Early Rising 130

THOMAS WILLIAM PARSONS. 1819–1892
Health and Wealth 132
Saint Valentine's Day 134
In Return for some Prairie Birds 135

JAMES RUSSELL LOWELL. 1819–1891
Auf Wiedersehen 136
Without and Within 138
Aladdin 140
An Ember Picture 141
The Nightingale in the Study 143
The Petition 146
In Arcadia 147

CONTENTS

THOMAS DUNN ENGLISH. 1819–1902   Page
    Kate Vane 150
WILLIAM WETMORE STORY. 1819–1895
    Do You Remember 152
    A Musical Box 155
    Snowdrop 157
JAMES THOMAS FIELDS. 1820–1881
    The Search 158
    Mabel, in New Hampshire 159
PETER REMSEN STRONG. 1822–1878
    "Awful!" 160
CHARLES GODFREY LELAND. 1824–1903
    Eva 162
    Thelemé 163
RICHARD HENRY STODDARD. 1825–1903
    The Flower of Love Lies Bleeding 166
    The Divan 168
JOHN TOWNSEND TROWBRIDGE. 1827–
    Pleasant Street 169
FITZ JAMES O'BRIEN. 1828–1862
    On the Passaic 173
CHARLES GRAHAM HALPINE. 1829–1868
    Feminine Arithmetic 175
    Quakerdom. The Formal Call 176
HENRY TIMROD. 1829–1867
    A Trifle 178
SILAS WEIR MITCHELL. 1829–
    A Decanter of Madeira 179
EDMUND CLARENCE STEDMAN. 1833–
    Pan in Wall Street 181
    Provençal Lovers 184
    Cousin Lucrece 186
    Fuit Ilium 189

CONTENTS

RICHARD REALF. 1834–1878   Page
    Sunbeam and I 193

GEORGE ARNOLD. 1834–1865
    Beer 195
    The Jolly Old Pedagogue 197
    Youth and Age 200

CHARLES HENRY WEBB. 1834–
    The King and the Pope 201
    Dictum Sapienti 203
    With a Rosebud 204
    With a Rose 205
    What she said about it 206
    Dum Vivimus Vigilamus 207

WILLIAM HENRY VENABLE. 1836–
    The School Girl 209
    The Tunes Dan Harrison used to Play . . . 211

THOMAS BAILEY ALDRICH. 1836–
    Nocturne 213
    Amontillado 214
    Thalia 216
    In an Atelier 218
    L' Eau Dormante 221
    On an Intaglio Head of Minerva 222

WILLIAM DEAN HOWELLS. 1837–
    The Thorn 224

MARY MAPES DODGE. 1838–
    The Minuet 225
    Over the Way 227
    Little Words 228

JOHN HAY. 1838–
    How it Happened 230

CONTENTS

BRET HARTE. 1839-1902   Page
    Miss Blanche Says 232
    Her Letter 236
    Dolly Varden 239
    What the Wolf Really Said to Little Red Riding-hood   241

AMELIA WALSTEIN CARPENTER. 1840–
    Old Flemish Lace 242

NORA PERRY. 1841-1896
    Sweet Sixteen 243
    The Love-Knot 245
    Yesterday 247

FREDERICK WADSWORTH LORING. 1848-1871
    The Old Professor 248

EDWARD ROWLAND SILL. 1841-1887
    Eve's Daughter 250

ANNIE DOUGLAS ROBINSON. [Marian Douglas.] 1842–
    Picture Poems for Young Folks 251

MARC COOK. [Vandyke Brown.] 1854-1882
    An Honest Confession 252
    Growing Old 255
    Her Opinion of the Play 257
    To a Pretty Schoolma'am 259

GEORGE WASHINGTON CABLE. 1844–
    An Editor's First-Born 261

RICHARD WATSON GILDER. 1844–
    A Midsummer Song 262

THEODORE PEASE COOK. 1844–
    Blue-beard 264

JOHN BOYLE O'REILLY. 1844-1890
    A White Rose 266
    An Art Master 267

CONTENTS

	Page
HENRY AUGUSTIN BEERS. 1847–	
A Shades	268
JAMES JEFFREY ROCHE. 1847–	
The V-A-S-E	269
WALTER LEARNED. 1847–	
Eheu! Fugaces	271
Cupid's Kiss	272
To Critics	273
Time's Revenge	274
FRANCIS SALTUS SALTUS. 1849–1889	
Pastel	275
GEORGE A. BAKER. 1849–	
Le Dernier Jour d'un Condamné	276
De Lunatico	278
HARRISON ROBERTSON. 1850–	
Appropriation	280
The Story of the Gate	282
EUGENE FIELD. 1850–1895	
Long Ago	284
Thirty-nine	286
Apple-Pie and Cheese	288
Old Times, Old Friends, Old Love	291
IRWIN RUSSELL. 1853–1879	
Cosmos	293
HENRY CUYLER BUNNER. 1855–1896	
The Way to Arcady	294
Candor	297
"One, Two, Three!"	298
The Chaperon	300
Forfeits	302
CHARLES HENRY LÜDERS. 1858–1891	
My Maiden Aunt	303

CONTENTS

RICHARD HOVEY. 1864–1900   Page
   A Toast 305
   The Love of a Boy—To-day 306

ANNE REEVE ALDRICH. 1866–1892
   Souvenirs 307
   Fanny 308

AMERICAN FAMILIAR VERSE

INTRODUCTION

I

"FAMILIAR VERSE" is the apt term Cowper preferred to describe the lyric of commingled sentiment and playfulness which is more generally and more carelessly called *vers de société*. The lyric of this sort is less emotional, or at least less expansive, than the regular lyric; and it seeks to veil the depth of its feeling behind a debonair assumption of gaiety. In fact its feeling must not be deep, since it is the exact opposite of the poetry of genuine inspiration. It cannot deal with the profounder passions, and " its light touch," so Bagehot declares, " is not competent to express eager, intense emotion." Familiar verse is in poetry closely akin to what in prose is known as the " eighteenth-century essay"; Prior and Gay were early representatives of the one, as Steele and Addison were the creators of the other. Familiar verse is a far better designation than *vers de société* for two reasons: first, because the use of a French phrase might seem to imply that these witty and graceful poems are more abundant in French literature than in English, — which is not the fact; and second, because, however light and bright these lyrics may be, they are not mere society-verses, with only the glitter and the emptiness of the fashionable parade. They are not the idle amusement of those

> Who tread with jaded step the weary mill —
> Grind at the wheel, and call it " pleasure " still;
> Gay without mirth, fatigued without employ,
> Slaves to the joyless phantom of a joy.

No doubt, social verse should have polish, and finish, and the well-bred ease of the man of the world; but it ought also to carry at least a suggestion of the more serious aspects of life. It should not be frothily frivolous or coldly cynical, any more than it should be broadly comic or boisterously funny. It is at liberty to hint at hidden tears, even when it seems to be wreathed in smiles. It has no right to parade mere cleverness; and it must shun all affectation, as it must avoid all self-consciousness. It should appear to possess a colloquial carelessness which is ever shrinking from the commonplace and which has succeeded in concealing every trace of that labor of the literary artist by which alone it has attained their seemingly spontaneous perfection.

"Familiar verse" is perhaps somewhat more exact than the term once employed by Mr. Stedman, — "patrician rhymes," which is a designation possibly a little chilly for these airy lyrics. To fall fully within the definition, so the late Frederick Locker-Lampson asserted, a poem must be brief and brilliant; and the late Tom Hood added that it ought also to be buoyant. Brevity, brilliancy, buoyancy, — these are qualities we cannot fail to find in the best of Locker-Lampson's own verses, in Praed's, in Prior's, — and also in Holmes's, in Lowell's, and in Bret Harte's.

INTRODUCTION

Brevity it must have first of all; and Locker-Lampson excluded the "Rape of the Lock" "on account of its length, which renders it much too important," although it "would otherwise be one of the finest specimens of *vers de société* in any language." Here it is permissible to echo the opinion of Poe, who held that a poem could scarcely exceed one hundred lines in length under penalty of losing its unity of impression. But, on the other hand, the poem of this species must not be excessively condensed, or else it is not important enough. A couplet does not give room to turn round in. Gay's

> Life is a jest, and all things show it;
> I said so once, and now I know it,

and Pope's

> I am his Highness' dog at Kew.
> Pray, sir, tell me, — whose dog are you?

have rather the sharp snap of the epigram than the gentler flow of genuine *vers de société*. And so certain of the slighter pieces in the Greek anthology, lovely as they are and exquisite, lack the modest amplitude fairly to be expected from a poem which claims admission into this charmed circle.

Brilliant it must be also; and this requirement excludes "Sally in Our Alley," for example, because it is "too homely and too entirely simple and natural"; and it keeps out "John Gilpin" as well, because it is too frankly comic in its intent, too boldly funny. But the brilliancy must not be excessive; and the diffused glow of the incandescent lamp is better than the sputtering glare of the arc light. If the brilliancy is attained by too violent and too obvious an effort, the light lyric is likely to harden into artificiality;

4 AMERICAN FAMILIAR VERSE

and this is a danger that even Praed does not always escape. His "Chaunt of the Brazen Head" has a lustre that is almost metallic; the sparkle is undeniable, but in time the insistent antithesis reveals itself as mechanical at least, not to call it either tricky or tiresome.

Buoyancy is the third requisite; and this is not so easy to define as the others. Yet its necessity is plain enough when we note how heavy certain metrical efforts may be, although they achieve brevity and even a superficial brilliance. They lack the final ease and the careless felicity; they are not wholly free from an awkwardness that is not unfairly to be termed lumbering. For example, buoyancy is just what is lacking in the rhyming epistle of John Wilson Croker "To Miss Peel on her Marriage" — quatrains which Locker-Lampson held in sufficient esteem to include in his carefully chosen "Lyra Elegantiarum" and which Mr. Swinburne despisingly dismissed as "twenty villainous lines."

Just as comedy is ever in danger of declining into farce (a mishap that has almost befallen the "Rivals," for example), or else of stiffening into the serious drama (a turning aside that is visible in "Froufrou"), so in like manner has familiar verse ever to avoid breadth of humor on the one side and depth of feeling on the other. It must eschew not merely coarseness or vulgarity, but even free and hearty laughter; and it must refrain from dealing not only with the soul-plumbing abysses of the tragic, but even with the ground-swell of any sweeping emotion. It must keep on the crest of the waves, midway between the utter triviality of the murmuring shallows and the silent profundity of the depths that are dumb.

INTRODUCTION

Perhaps this is one reason why so few of these brevet-poems have been the work of the greater wits or of the greater poets; familiar verse is too serious to carry all the fun of the jesters and too slight to convey the more solemn message of the major bards. Rather has it been the casual recreation of true lyrists not in the front rank; or else it has been the sudden excursion of those not reckoned among the songsters, often men of the world, for once achieving in verse a seeming spontaneity, like that which gives zest to a delightful conversation.

Perhaps again this is a reason why *vers de société* can be found flourishing most luxuriantly when the man of the world is himself most abundant and when he has helped to set up an ideal of sparkling nimbleness in the give-and-take of social encounter. "When society ceases to be simple, it becomes sceptical," and when it "becomes refined, it begins to dread the exhibition of strong feeling; —" so wrote one of the reviewers of Locker-Lampson's collection; and "in such an atmosphere, emotion takes refuge in jest, and passion hides itself in scepticism of passion." And the reviewer added that there is a delicious piquancy in the poets who represent this social mood, and who are put in a class apart by "the way they play bo-peep with their feelings."

In the stately sentences of his time the elder Disraeli declared that in the production of *vers de société*,

"genius will not always be sufficient to impart that grace of amenity which seems peculiar to those who are accustomed to elegant society. These productions are more the effusions of taste than genius, and it is not sufficient that the poet is inspired by the Muse, he must also suffer his concise page to be polished by the hand of the Graces."

6   AMERICAN FAMILIAR VERSE

Locker-Lampson maintained that

"the tone should not be pitched high; it should be idiomatic, and rather in the conversational key; the rhythm should be crisp and sparkling, and the rhyme frequent and never forced, while the entire poem should be marked by tasteful moderation, high finish, and completeness: for, however trivial the subject-matter may be, indeed rather in proportion to its triviality, subordination to the rules of composition and perfection of execution should be strictly enforced."

And Mr. Austin Dobson drawing up "Twelve Good Rules" for the writer of familiar verse advised him to be "colloquial but not commonplace," to be as witty as he liked, to be "serious by accident," and to be "pathetic with the greatest discretion."

II

THE limitations of familiar verse being thus clearly indicated, the qualities to be demanded being plainly declared, and the defects to be avoided being sharply set forth, it is possible now to consider the history of the species as this has established itself in the English language both in Great Britain and in the United States, and to inquire whether it has not analogues at least in the other modern tongues and also in the two classical literatures.

Those who may search Greek literature for frequent examples of familiar verse are doomed to disappointment and even in the lovely lyrics of the "Anthology," so human, so sad, so perfect in precision of phrase, we fail to find the lightness, the playfulness, the gaiety of true *vers de société*. We note brevity nearly always, brilliancy sometimes, and even buoyancy occasionally; we mark a lapidary concision that only Landor, of all the moderns, was ever able to achieve; but we feel that the tone is a little too grave and a little too austere. Perhaps the Greek spirit was too simple and too lofty to stoop to the pleasantry and prettiness of familiar verse. Perhaps the satiric reaction against excessive romanticism, which sustains so much modern *vers de société*, was not possible before the birth of romance itself. Perhaps, indeed, the banter and the gently satiric playfulness of social verse was not to be expected in a race, no matter how gifted it might be lyrically, which kept woman in social inferiority and denied her the social privileges that give to modern society its charm and its variety.

At first glance it would seem as though more than one lyric of Anacreon at least, and perhaps of Theocritus also, ought to fall well within the most rigid definition of familiar verse. But there is scarcely a single poem of Anacreon's which really approaches the type we are seeking. The world for which he wrote reveals itself as very narrow; and he is found to be devoid of "catholicity of human interest," as Tom Hood asserted. His verses are a little lacking in tenderness of sentiment; and as Professor Jebb says, Anacreon's "sensuousness is tempered merely by intellectual charm," — and this is not what we require in social verse.

Theocritus also, exquisite as are his vignettes of Alexandrian life, perfect as they are in tone and feeling, clear cut as an intaglio and delightful as a Tanagra figurine, — Theocritus is at once too idyllic and too realistic. His verses are without certain of the characteristics which are imperative in true *vers de société*. They are at once a little too homely and a little too poetic. If a selection from Greek literature was absolutely imperative, probably a copy of verses combining brevity, brilliancy, and buoyancy could be found more easily among the scanty lyrics of Agathias or of Antipater than amid the larger store of Theocritus or of Anacreon.

Perhaps it is the more prominent position of woman in Rome which makes a search in Latin literature a more certain pleasure. Yet the world in which Catullus lived, that "tenderest of Roman poets nineteen hundred years ago," while it was externally most luxurious, had an underlying rudeness and an ill-concealed coarseness. And Catullus himself, with all his nimble wit, his scholarly touch, his instinctive certainty of taste, was consumed by too fierce a flame of passion to be satisfied often with the leisurely interweaving of jest and earnest which we look for in the songster of society. Only too infrequently does he allow himself the courtly grace of familiar verse, — as he does in his "Dedication for a Volume of Lyrics"; in his "Invitation to Dinner" and in his "Morning Call," so sympathetically paraphrased by Landor.

Half a generation later we come to Horace, a perfect master of the lighter lyric. He has the wide knowledge of a man of the world and the consummate ease of an accomplished craftsman in verse. He can achieve both the "curious felicity" and the "art that hides itself." And his tone, so Walter Bagehot insisted,

" is that of prime ministers; the easy philosophy is that of courts and parliaments. . . . He is but the extreme and perfect type of a whole class of writers, some of whom exist in every literary age, and who give expression to what we may call the poetry of equanimity, — that is, the world's view of itself, its self-satisfaction, its conviction that you must hear what comes, not hope for much, think *some* evil, never be excited, admire little, and then you will be at peace."

Perhaps this view of Horace's philosophy is a little too disenchanted; but Bagehot here suggested why this Roman poet was likely to be one of the masters of familiar verse; and it is Horace's catholicity of human interest, even more than his naturalness, which makes his lines sometimes so startlingly modern. It was easy for Thackeray to find London equivalents for the Latin "Persicos odi," and for Molière earlier, and Mr. Austin Dobson later, to imitate "Donec gratus." But there is little need to cite further, for no poet has tempted more adapters and translators, — not always indeed to his profit, and in fact often to their undoing, since it is only by an inspiration as happy as the original that any modern may hope to equal the sureness of stroke characteristic of a poet who shunned the remote adjective and who showed himself ever content with the vocabulary of every day.

It is not pleasant to pass down from the benign rule of Augustus to the tyranny of Nero, and to contrast the constant manliness of Horace with the servility of Martial, a servility finding relief now and again in the utmost bitterness of unrestrained invective. Horace, with all his equanimity, was never indifferent to ideas, and he had an ethical code of his own; but Martial rarely revealed even a hint of moral feeling. He was cynical of necessity: and therefore is he habitually too hard and too rasping to attain the geniality which belongs to the better sort of social verse. Few of his poems are really long enough to be styled lyrics; and the vast majority are merely epigrams, with the wilful condensation and the arbitrary pointedness, that have been the bane of the epigram ever since Martial set the bad example. But even though the Latin poet, as Professor Mackail asserts, made his strongest appeal "to all that was worst in Roman taste, — its heavy-handedness, its admiration of verbal cleverness, its tendency towards brutality," still now and again it is possible to pick out a poem that falls fairly within the definition of familiar verse, — "In habentem amaenas aedes," for example.

III

WHEN at last we pass over the long suspension-bridge that arches the dark gulf between the ancient world and the modern, we discover that the more direct inheritors of the Latin tradition, the Italians and the Spaniards, have neither of them contributed abundantly to this special department of lyric poetry. It may be that the Spanish language is too grandiloquent and too sonorous to be readily playful; and perhaps the Spanish character itself is either too loftily dignified or too realistically shrewd to be able often to achieve that harmonious blending of the grave and the gay which is essential in familiar verse. It is true that Lope de Vega, early master of every form of the drama and bold adventurer into every other realm of literature, has left us a few poems that might demand inclusion; and among them is an ingenious sonnet on the difficulty of making a sonnet, which was cleverly Englished by the late H. C. Bunner and which may have suggested to Voiture his more famous rondeau, adroitly imitated by Mr. Austin Dobson. No doubt there are a few other Spanish poets—Gil Vicente, for one—who might be enlisted as contributors to an international anthology of *vers de société;* but the fact remains that the

INTRODUCTION

Spanish section of any such collection would be slighter even than the Italian.

And the Italian contribution would not be very important, in spite of the national facility in improvisation, — or perhaps because of this dangerous gift. In the earlier Italian Renascence existence seems to have been almost too strenuous for social verse. As we call the roll of the Italian poets, we may note the name of more than one master of the passionate lyric and of the scorching satire, but we find scarcely any writer who has left us verses of the requisite brevity, brilliancy, and buoyancy. In Rossetti's "Dante and his Circle" there is more than one poem that seems to have this triple qualification, although on more careful examination the sentiment is seen to be too sincere and too frankly expressed, or else the tone is too rarely playful to warrant any liberal selection from these fascinating pages. Perhaps even from this volume a more lively little piece might here and there be borrowed, such for instance as Sacchetti's catch "On a Wet Day." A little later there is Berni, whose metrical portrait of himself might fairly be compared — and not altogether to its disadvantage — with one or another of Praed's caressingly tender sketches of character. The Italians have no lack of biting epigram and of pertinent pasquinade; and they excel in broad burlesque and in laughable parody. But the mock-heroic, however clever it may be, is not the same as *vers de société*. And even in the nineteenth century, where there was a firmer social solidarity, the only name which forces itself on our attention is that of Giusti, — whose idiomatic ballads have not unfairly been likened to the songs of Béranger.

The more northern languages are less likely to reward research, partly because of the prolonged rudeness of the Teutonic tongues and partly because of the more rigid seriousness of the folk that speak them. There is a true lyric grace in the songs of the Minnesingers, despite their frequent artificiality; but they again are too direct and too purely lyric. However ingenious they may be, they are without the wit and the humor which we look for in familiar verse. Even the later and far greater Goethe, who, for all his Olympian serenity, revealed at times the possession of that specific levity which is a prerequisite for the songster of society, — even Goethe chose to condense his wit into the distichs of his "Xenien" rather than to commingle it with his balladry. He himself thought it strange that with all he had done, there was no one of his poems "that would suit the Lutheran hymn-book"; and it is perhaps even stranger that scarcely any one of them would suit such an anthology as has been here suggested. Perhaps a claim might be made for his "Ergo Bibamus," which has almost briskness enough to warrant its acceptance.

From Heine, of course, a choice would be less difficult; and both the "Widow and the Daughter" and the "Grammar of the Stars" seem to meet all the requirements. But affluent as Heine is in sentiment and master as he is both of girding satire and of airy persiflage, there is ever a heart-break to be heard in his verses, — an unforgettable sob. The chords of his lyre are really too deep and too resonant for him to chant trifles. The "brave soldier in the war of liberation of humanity," as he styled himself, even in his paraded mockery and in his irrepressible wit, was really too much in earnest to happen often on the happy mean which makes familiar verse a possibility.

INTRODUCTION

IV

In the French language, at last, the seeker after *vers de société* finds not only the name, but the thing itself, the real thing; and he finds it in abundance and of the best quality. Some part of this abundance is due, no doubt, to the French tongue itself, for, as a shrewd writer has reminded us, " a language long employed by a delicate and critical society is a treasury of dextrous felicities"; it may not be what Emerson finely called " fossil poetry," but it is " crystallized *esprit.*" Society-verse might be expected to flourish most luxuriantly among a people governed by the social instinct as the French are, and keenly appreciative of the social qualities. The French invented the *salon*, which is the true hot-house for familiar verse; and they have raised both correspondence and conversation to the dignity of fine arts. As we scan the history of the past three centuries we note that in France society and literature have met on terms that approach equality far more nearly than in any other country. The French men of letters have often been men of the world, even if the French men of the world have been men of letters no more frequently than the English.

Moreover it is in prose rather than in poetry that the French have achieved their amplest triumphs. Whatever reservations an English reader must make in his praise of French poetry, he need make none in his eulogy of French prose. In prose the French have commonly a perfection to which the English language can pretend only too rarely. Their prose has order and balance and harmony; it flows limpidly with a charming transparency; it is ever lucid, ever flexible, ever various; it has at once an obvious polish and an apparent ease. And to these precious qualifications for a form of poetry, seemingly so unambitious as social verse, must be added the possession not only of the wit and the vivacity which are acknowledged characteristics of the French, but also their ownership of something far more needful, — the gift of comedy.

"For many years the French have not been more celebrated for memoirs which professedly describe a real society than they have been for the light social song which embodies its sentiments and pours forth its spirit," said Walter Bagehot, writing in the middle of the nineteenth century. He maintained that the French mind had a genius for the poetry of society because it had "the quickest insight into the exact relation of surrounding superficial phenomena." He held that the spirit of these lighter lyrics is ever half mirthful and that they cannot produce a profound impression. "A gentle pleasure, half sympathy, half amusement, is that at which they aim," he suggested; adding that, "they do not please us equally in all moods of mind: sometimes they seem nothing and nonsense, — like society itself."

Perhaps it is in consequence of the prosaic element perceptible in much of their more pretentious poetry that the French themselves have not considered curiously their own familiar verse. While there are nearly half-a-dozen collections of the *vers de société* of the English language, a diligent seeking has failed to find a single similar anthology in French. A book of *ballades* there is, but the most of these are serious in tone rather than serio-comic; the pertest of the many epigrammatic quatrains of the language have been gathered into an engaging little volume; but a selection of the best of their lighter lyrics, having

INTRODUCTION

brevity, brilliancy, and buoyancy, has not yet been undertaken by any French critic, although he would have only the embarrassment of choosing from out a superabundance of enticing examples.

For the most part the vigorous verse of Villon, that warm "voice from the slums of Paris," has too poignant a melancholy to be included, for all its bravado gaiety; and though he tries to carry it off with a laugh, the disreputable poet fails to disguise the depth of his feeling. And yet it would be impossible to exclude the famous "Ballade of Old-Time Ladies" with its unforgettable refrain, "Where are the snows of yester-year?" A larger selection would be easier from Villon's contemporary, Charles of Orleans, longtime a prisoner in England, — a poet far less energetic and not so disenchanted, but possessing by birth "the manners and tone of good society." Stevenson especially praised his rondels for their "inimitable lightness and delicacy of touch" and declared that the royal lyrist's "lines go with a lilt and sing themselves to music of their own."

The rondel was the fixed form in which Charles of Orleans was most often successful, although he frequently attempted the ballade also. This larger form the later Clément Marot managed with assured mastery. One of the best known of his more playful poems is the *ballade à double refrain* setting forth the duplicity of "Brother Lubin," — a poem which has been rendered into English both by Bryant and Longfellow, although neither of them held himself bound by the strict letter of the law that prescribes the limitation and the ordering of the rhymes properly to be expected in the ballade. As it happens the American poets were not happily inspired in rendering this characteristic specimen of Marot's discreet raillery and metrical agility; and in their versions we fail to find the limpid lines and the polished irony of the French poet, who was able so easily to marry the elegant with the natural,— qualities rarely conjoined, even in French. And yet Locker-Lampson was able to paraphrase one of Clément Marot's lesser lyrics, "Du Rys de Madame d'Allebert," with indisputable felicity.

Space fails here to select familiar verse from out the poems of Ronsard and Du Bellay and Desportes or to excerpt cautiously from the later poetasters who were forever rhyming in the ruelles of the *précieuses* and who clubbed together to go on record in the celebrated "Guirlande à Julie." But Corneille and Molière and La Fontaine cannot be treated in this cavalier fashion. Taine calls La Fontaine's epistles to Madame de Sablière "little masterpieces of respectful gallantry and delicate tenderness." It is this same note of tender gallantry which strikes us in the poems which Molière and Corneille severally addressed to the handsome and alluring actress, Mademoiselle Du Parc. Corneille's stanzas are almost too elevated in tone to permit them to be termed familiar verse; and yet when they are read in the English rendering of Locker-Lampson they do not transcend the modest boundaries of this minor department of poetry.

In the eighteenth century we come to Dufresny, with his "Morrows," a little comedy in four quatrains, to Piron, rather more inclined to the pert and pungent epigram than to the more suave and gracious song of society; and to Voltaire, the arch-wit of the age, accomplished in social verse as in every other conceivable form of literary endeavor. Perhaps it was of Voltaire that Lowell was thinking when he asserted that in French poetry only "the high polish kept out the decay." Yet it was Lowell himself who rendered into flowing English an epistle of Voltaire's to Madame Du Chatelet, — stanzas in which the aging wit refers to his years, not so touchingly as Corneille had done, it is true, but with dignity none the less.

In the nineteenth century it is possible to perceive two diverging tendencies in French *vers de société*, one of them being rather more obviously literary in its manner and including certain of the more piquant lyrics of Hugo, Musset and Gautier, while the other is somewhat humbler in its aim and seemingly simpler in its execution. To this second group belong the best of Béranger's ballads, of Gustave Nadaud's, and of Henry Mürger's. Of Nadaud the one perfect example is "Carcassonne," so sympathetically Englished by John R. Thompson; and of Mürger probably the most characteristic, — in its presentation of the actual atmosphere of that Bohemia which is truly a desert country by the sea, — is the lyric of "Old Loves," ingeniously paraphrased by Mr. Andrew Lang.

Goethe once declared that Béranger's songs "may he looked upon as the best things in their kind, especially when you observe the burden, without which they would be almost too earnest, too pointed and too epigrammatic for songs." And Goethe saw in Béranger a certain likeness to Horace and to Hafiz "who stood in the same way above their times, satirically and playfully setting forth the corruption of manners." Béranger is like Horace not only in his geniality and in his freedom from cynicism, but also in that he has tempted countless English translators, — mostly to their own undoing. At first glance it may appear that poetry so easy to read as Horace's or Béranger's, so direct, so unaffected, ought to be transferable into another tongue without great difficulty. But this appearance is altogether deceptive, and those who carelessly venture upon translation soon discover that all unwillingly they have been paying the highest compliment to the skill with which the metrical artist has succeeded in concealing his consummate craftsmanship. Even Thackeray, with all his cleverness, with all his understanding of Parisian life, did not achieve the impossible feat of making a wholly satisfactory English translation of a song of Béranger's, although he twice attempted the " Roi d'Yvetot," and although he did not fail to bring over into English not a little of the sentiment and of the sparkle of the " Grenier." Indeed it is this ballad of Béranger's which satisfies the definition of familiar verse more completely perhaps than any other piece of that Epicurean songster's.

A true lyric, whether ballad or sonnet or elegy, is not addressed to the eye alone; it is ever intended to be said or sung. The songs of Béranger are real songs, fitted to a tune already running in the head of the lyrist; and they have in fact sung themselves into being. The poems of Hugo and Gautier and Musset, even when they are most lyrical, are rather for recitation or reading aloud; they are not intended for the actual accompaniment of music. Once indeed Musset gave us a lyric, which is not only singable, but which seems to insist on an alliance with music. This single song is the " Mimi Pinson " with its exquisite commingling of wit and melancholy. For the most part the stanzas of Musset are too full of fire and ardor to be classed as familiar verse; they have too rich a note of passion; and despite their brilliance they are of a truth too sad.

It is only occasionally also that a poem of Hugo's

falls within the scope of this inquiry. His was too large an utterance for mere social verse; and the melody of his varied rhythms is too vibrating. His legends are epic in their breadth; and he lacks the unliterary simplicity and the vernacular terseness of familiar verse. For all his genius he is deficient not only in wit and in humor but even in the sense-of-humor; and there is some truth in Heine's jibe that Victor Hugo's "muse had two left hands."

From the treasury of "Enamels and Cameos," there is only the embarrassment of choosing, as no French poet has written poems more translucent than Théophile Gautier. His is the clear serenity of temper and the unfailing certainty of stroke which reveal the master of social verse. But the French poet's invincible dexterity is the despair of the translator. How render into another language the firmly chiseled stanzas of a lyrist who was enamored of the vocabulary and who was ever wooing it ardently and successfully? As Mr. Henry James says, Gautier "loved words for themselves, — for their look, their aroma, their color, their fantastic intimations." Locker-Lampson accomplished the almost impossible feat of finding English equivalents for Gautier's French, — in the first two quatrains of "A Winter Fantasy"; — but even he thought it best to end his own poem in his own way. Probably the translation that most triumphantly carries over into English the finest essence of Gautier's art is Mr. Swinburne's "We are in love's land to-day."

V

THE fact that a language may lack a satisfactory word to describe a certain thing is not always a proof that the people using the tongue are in reality deprived of that for which they may have no name of their own. In English, for example, there is no exact equivalent for the French *ennui;* — but who would be so bold as to question the British possession of this state of mind, although it may be nameless in their speech? In French, again, there is no single word connoting all the shades of meaning contained in *home;* — and yet no race is more home-keeping than the French and no other nation has more sharply recognized in its laws the solidarity of the family. And although the most usual term for familiar verse is *vers de société*, there is little doubt that English literature, taking into account both its branches, British and American, is at least as rich in this minor department of poetry as French literature may be. Indeed, the more carefully the social verse of the English language is compared with that of the French language, the more probable appears to be the superiority of the *vers de société* in our own tongue, — a superiority not only in abundance but also in variety.

The French, as has been noted, have never been moved to bring together in a single volume the most characteristic of their lighter lyrics; and the absence of an adequate anthology makes it hard for a foreigner to assure himself that he is really acquainted with the best the French have to offer. But in English, as it happens, there is an anthology which is wholly satisfactory; and the finest examples of familiar verse, from the beginnings of our literature down

INTRODUCTION

to the middle of the nineteenth century, have been collected in the "Lyra Elegantiarium" of the late Frederick Locker-Lampson. With this volume in his hand it is easy even for the careless reader to perceive that the store of social verse in England is both ample and many-sided, — despite the fact that we are in the habit of borrowing a French name to describe it.

By excluding the work of all writers living when his volume was first issued, now nearly twoscore years ago, Locker-Lampson deprived his readers of any selections from his own "London Lyrics" from Calverley's "Fly-Leaves," from Mr. Lang's "Ballades in Blue China," and from Mr. Austin Dobson's "Vignettes in Rhyme." He was also forced to leave out nearly all that was best in the books of our early American writers, for the leaders of American literature were fortunately surviving when the British anthologist was at work on his collection. But even without making allowance for these self-imposed restrictions, the social verse collected by Locker-Lampson is remarkably fine; its average is surprisingly high and its range is astonishingly wide. And it shows that English literature from the days of Skelton and Sidney down to Hood and Thackeray in the middle of the nineteenth century, was illumined not only by great poets of lofty imagination and of sweeping power, but also by a host of minor bards who were able to "express more or less well the lighter desires of human nature," as Bagehot phrases it, "those that have least of unspeakable depth, partake most of what is perishable and earthly, and least of the immortal soul." These minor bards were masters in their own way and they were able to give their little masterpieces the brevity, the brilliancy, and the buoyancy which we expect in the best familiar verse.

Nor are the minor bards the sole contributors to "Lyra Elegantiarium." Not a few of the most characteristic pieces in Locker-Lampson's collection are from the works of the greater poets, the mighty songsters who are the glory of our literature. There is one poem of Shakspere's, "O Mistress Mine, Where are you roaming"; and there are three of Ben Jonson's, including the lovely lyric, "To Celia,"—

> Drink to me only with thine eyes,
> And I will pledge with mine;
> Or leave a kiss but in the cup
> And I'll not look for wine.

There are three selections from Dryden, and there might easily have been more. There is one from Gray, — the delightful lines "On the death of a favorite cat." There are five by Byron and six by Coleridge; there is one by Wordsworth and another by Scott; and there are thirty-eight by Landor, "whose lightest and slightest claim to immortality," so Mr. Swinburne has asserted with his wonted and wanton exaggeration, "is his indistinguishable supremacy over all possible competitors as a writer of social or occasional verse, more bright, more graceful, more true in tone, more tender in expression, more deep in suggestion, more delicate in touch, than any possible Greek or Latin or French or English rivals."

Not only have the greater poets now and again condescended to the familiar verse in which success is almost as rare as it is in the loftier lyric, but the masters of prose have often been willing to adventure themselves as songsters of society. Among the dramatists, Congreve and Sheridan, of course, and

INTRODUCTION 23

Etherege and Vanbrugh as well, proved that upon occasion they could rhyme with the requisite facility and felicity. Of the novelists, both Smollett and Fielding more than once attempted to turn a couplet with playful intent. The politicians especially have been prone to seize on social verse as a precious relaxation from their sterner labors; and by no means the least interesting or the least admirable of the examples in Locker-Lampson's collection are the work of Chesterfield and the Walpoles, — both Robert and Horace, — of Canning and of Fox. The first Lord Houghton it was who suggested that " the faculty of writing verse (quite apart from poetic genius) is the most delightful of literary accomplishments, and it almost always carries with it the more generally useful gift of writing good prose." And it may be that the gift of writing good prose carries with it the likelihood that its possessor may achieve distinction in the special department of poetry where vernacular terseness is ever a most valuable qualification.

But what the prose writers and the greater poets have chanced to achieve in this variety of lyric, charming as it may be and unexpectedly exquisite, is after all a smaller contribution to our store of social verse than that which we have received from the half-dozen or the half-score lyrists who have won the most of their fame by their essays in familiar verse. In any history of *vers de société* in the British islands attention must be concentrated on Herrick and Prior, on Cowper and Goldsmith, on Praed and Hood, on Moore and Thackeray, and on Locker-Lampson and Austin Dobson.

It was in one of his juvenile essays that Lowell called Herrick " the best and most unconscious of the song-writers of his tuneful time." The best he is, no doubt; but is he really unconscious? Is it not rather that by a perfected art he could achieve spontaneity and the appearance of unconsciousness? Never do his unaffected lyrics reveal the long labor of the file; but who can guess what hidden toil underlay the lightest of his lovely trifles? Though they may never smell of the lamp, but seem rather to have flowered on a spring morning and of their own volition, it would be rash indeed to deem Herrick only an improvisor. There is the odor of an old-time garden in his fragrant rhymes, — an echo of mating birds in the liquid melody of his varied measures. Waller's lines "On a Girdle," Carew's "Prayer to the Wind," Suckling's "Ballad on a Wedding," Lovelace's lyric on "Going to the Wars," — none of these excel Herrick's "Gather ye Rose-Buds while ye may" in imponderable grace or in incomparable ease. And nowhere is there a metrical perfection more certain, a play of fancy more captivating than in the "Bride-Cake," and in "Delight in Disorder."

In Prior's familiar verse there is more of coarseness than there is in Herrick's — since the latter revealed his grosser likings chiefly in his epigrams. In Prior, again, there is a cynicism of tone, especially in regard to woman, of which there is no trace in Herrick's brightsome balladry. But not a few of the foremost of Prior's pieces are as unstained as they are unaffected. Cowper, — and no English poet ever had a better right to be heard on this subject — asserted that "every man conversant with verse-writing knows, and knows by painful experience, that the familiar style is of all styles the most difficult to succeed in. To make verse speak the language of prose, without being prosaic, to marshal the words of it in such an order as they might naturally take in falling from the lips of an extemporary speaker, yet without meanness, harmoniously, elegantly, and without seeming to displace a syllable for the sake of the rhyme, is one of the most arduous tasks a poet can undertake. He that could accomplish this task was Prior; many have imitated his excellence in this particular, but the best copies have fallen far short of the original." A past master Prior is of graceful gaiety, of debonair raillery, of jaunty audacity; and yet he may be found a little lacking in true feeling sometimes, in tenderness, if not in sincerity. But there is no denying his exhibition of all these qualities in what must be considered as his most perfect poem, — " To a child of quality five years old.

Cowper and Goldsmith loom larger among the lesser British bards than some who have been admitted to the sacred heights solely because of their familiar verse; yet it is not by their most important works or by their most pretentious that they are now best known or best beloved. The careless ballad of "John Gilpin" is likely to outlive the solid translation of the " Iliad "; and " Retaliation" will probably outlast the " Deserted Village." Humor and good humor are found together in the familiar verse of both Cowper and Goldsmith, unlike as were the men themselves. Playful and cheerful are the " Jackdaw" that Cowper took over from the Latin, and the "Elegy on Mrs. Mary Blaise" which Goldsmith lightly borrowed from the French; and this playful cheerfulness is not so common that the verse it characterizes is likely soon to slip into oblivion. Nowadays, when more than a century stretches between us and the old-fashioned didacticism of Cowper and Goldsmith, the " Task" may be left unattempted except by professed students of poetry; and the "Traveller" may rest from his wanderings, reposing at last upon a dusty shelf. But there is still pleasure to be had in the perusal of the lines, "On the Death of Mrs. Throckmorton's Bullfinch"; and the "Haunch of Venison" still provides a feast for all who relish mischievous fun.

To-day the most ambitious poems of Moore seem sadly faded and outworn; even in his songs, where "all is beautiful, soft, half-sincere," as has been remarked, "there is a little falsetto in the tone; everything reminds you of the drawing-room and the pianoforte." And setting aside some of the simplest and most singable of his "Irish Melodies," the best of Moore that now survives is a little group of society-verses, dealing aptly and piquantly with the tinkle of the pianoforte and with the chatter of the drawing-room. There is more than a Dresden-china prettiness in "Lesbia hath a charming eye" and in "Farewell! — but whenever you welcome the hour." There is more than mere sparkle, there is feeling, superficial perhaps, but sincere as far as it goes, in his verses "To Bessy."

Hood's possession of pure pathos and also of frisky humor cannot be denied; but more often than not he preferred to display these qualities separately. Although his verse can be on occasion crisp and brisk, as in "I'm not a single man" and "Please to ring the belle," he did not often try to attain the rare balance of fun and sentiment which is expected in familiar verse and which Thackeray achieved so frequently. There is a frolicsome tenderness and a gentle sparkle about the "Mahogany Tree" and about the "Ballad of Bouillabaise" which is characteristically Thackerayan. The rhythm is free and flowing, the rhymes are ingenious and frequent; and the humor is external while the pathos is internal. The smile wreathes the corners of the lip while the tear is held back beneath the eyelid. Bolder than these is "Peg of Limavaddy" and deeper yet are the lines on the "Album and the Pen."

Thackeray derives from Cowper and from Goldsmith; while it is rather from Prior that Praed descends. Thackeray's verses are suave and suggestive; Praed's are sometimes a little hard; they have a luster that is almost metallic, and their vivacity is now and then almost too vigorous. But how certain the stroke is! How sharp the wit! How happy the rhyme! His portraits of persons are etchings rather than miniatures, and every feature is keenly limned. Even if his manner is at times a trifle mechanical, his antithesis unduly insisted upon, and his epigram over-emphatic, his wit is ever unflagging, his style is ever pelucid, and his rhythm is unfailingly dextrous and flexible. His radiance is rather that of the diamond than of the running brook; but the stone is always clear cut and highly polished and appropriately set. Mr. Austin Dobson has singled out "My Own Araminta" as a characteristic example of Praed's more sparkling lyrics and the "Vicar" as a satisfactory representative of his "more pensive character-pieces."

Mr. Austin Dobson is one of the two British bards whose supremacy in familiar verse was undisputed and indisputable in the final decade of the nineteenth century; and the other was the late Frederick Locker-Lampson. While Mr. Dobson derived his descent rather from Herrick, and, it may be, from Landor, Locker-Lampson had found his immediate model in Praed; and thus it happens that the "London Lyrics" of the latter fall more completely within the narrower limits of *vers de société* than do the "Vignettes in Rhyme" of the former. Locker-Lampson's "Piccadilly" and his "St. James's Street" are truly songs of Society with all the elegance and all the courtesy the fashionable world believes itself entitled to expect. Mr. Austin Dobson's "Molly Trefusis" and his "Ladies of St. James's" are a little larger in their appeal, as though the poet had a broader outlook on life and refused to allow himself to be confined wholly within the contracting circle of Society.

Locker-Lampson can be as witty as Praed, though his wit is less obtrusive and his cleverness is less often paraded. He is far more tender and his touch is more caressing; and yet it is with Praed and with Prior that he is to be classed and compared. Mr. Austin Dobson is more of a poet; he has a lyric note of his own purer and deeper than any we can catch in their verses; and so it is that he is less at ease than they are within the limitations of social verse and that his finest poems are some of them not fairly to be considered as familiar verse. Indeed, it is not with Praed and Prior that Mr. Dobson is to be measured, but rather with their teachers in versification; and not without warrant did Mr. Aldrich once declare that Mr. Dobson "has the grace of Suckling and the finish of Herrick, and is easily master of both in metrical art."

VI

It is only toward the end of the eighteenth century that a division begins to be observable in the broadening stream of English literature and that it thereafter runs in two channels, British and American.

INTRODUCTION

Of course, whatsoever is written in the English language belongs to English literature, if only it attains to the requisite individuality and the needful elevation; and yet, almost as soon as there came into existence such a thing as American literature, not long after the people of the United States had severed their political connection with Great Britain, the writings of American authors revealed certain minor characteristics unlike those of the British authors who were their contemporaries. It is not easy to declare precisely what it is that differentiates the American literature of the nineteenth century from the British literature of the same hundred years; nevertheless there are few critics who have failed to perceive the existence of this difference, even if the most of them have been unable to analyze it. As we here in the United States do not live under social conditions exactly like those acceptable to our kin across the sea, the more closely our literature is related to our own life, the more it must differ from that produced in the British Isles, despite the use of the same language and despite the inheritance of the same traditions.

This difference between American literature and British literature, unmistakable as it may be to many of us, is never very pronounced; and it is probably far less obvious in familiar verse than it is in poetry of a loftier aspiration. Perhaps this is due to the fact that the songsters of society must needs be bound by the customs and the conventions of well-bred circles, which will differ only a little no matter what the divergence of the latitude. The manners of Murray Hill cannot vary very much from those of Mayfair; and, indeed, the chief distinction between the familiar verse of the two countries is that the American poets have been less interested in Murray Hill than the British poets have been in Mayfair. In other words, American *vers de société* is less often a song of Society itself than is its British rival; it has a little less of the mere glitter of wit and perhaps a little more of the mellower tenderness of humor. It shrinks less from a homely theme; and it does not so often seek that flashing sharpness of outline, which Praed delighted in and which sometimes suggests fireworks at midnight.

As might be supposed, the sparse specimens of familiar verse produced on this side of the Atlantic, while the future United States were still colonies of Great Britain, have the usual characteristics of all colonial literatures and reveal a close imitation of models imported from the mother-country. Even the satire of the revolutionary period, pointed as it is and piquant, and far more frequent than is generally known, has scant originality of form. The "Battle of the Kegs" had British exemplars; and "McFingal" owed much to the example of Butler and of Churchill. Except that a plangent note of personal experience — and of love of nature also — is heard in it, now and again, the vigorous verse of Freneau varies but little from that produced by his British contemporaries. And yet a handful of familiar verse may be gleaned even in this rather barren field; and more than one of Freneau's playful poems, the "Parting Glass," for instance, and the cheerful lines "To a Caty-did" may keep company with a few other clever lyrics of this lighter sort to be chosen carefully from out the more solid metrical efforts of Thomas Evans, William Clifton, Royall Tyler, and John Quincy Adams.

Joel Barlow was the chief of the brave bards who wished to discount the future and who sought most ambitiously to celebrate the coming glories of this country; and it is a curious instance of the irony of time that while Barlow's "Columbiad," is as unreadable to-day — or at least as little read — as Timothy Dwight's "Conquest of Canaan," his unpretending rhymes in honor of the "Hasty-Pudding" are as fresh now, as lively, as amusing, as they were on the day they were penned. This sole surviving specimen of Barlow's poetic aspiration may incline a little too much toward the mock-heroic to fall completely within the definition of familiar verse; and it is a little lacking in the pathos which Thackeray infused into the " Ballad of Bouillabaise." But the sincerity of Barlow's lines is as undeniable as their cleverness, their shrewdness, and their common-sense: —

> There are who strive to stamp with disrepute
> The luscious food, because it feeds the brute;
> In tropes of high-strain'd wit, while gaudy prigs
> Compare thy nursling man to pamper'd pigs;
> With sovereign scorn I treat the vulgar jest,
> Nor fear to share thy bounties with the beast.
> What though the generous cow gives me to quaff
> The milk nutritious; am I then a calf?
> Or can the genius of the noisy swine,
> Though nursed on pudding, thence lay claim to mine.
> Sure the sweet song I fashion to thy praise,
> Runs more melodious than the notes they raise.

The reputation of the "Croaker Papers" of Halleck and Drake is sadly dimmed nowadays; and the reader in search of true *vers de société* is sadly disappointed, since he finds in them only *vers d'occasion* the interest of which has departed with the changing years. They are "songs of dead seasons," to use Mr. Swinburne's phrase; and the most of these jocular lyrics of the collaborating bards which seemed so clever and so pointed when New York was only a tiny town on the toe of Manhattan, are seen to-day to be so thickly studded with contemporary allusions that they are readable only with the aid of plentiful annotation,—and what is the zest of a joke that needs a footnote to be visible? In fact, nothing of Halleck's or Drake's, whether written by either singly or by both in collaboration, has revealed so vigorous a vitality as the charming and fanciful "Visit from St. Nicholas" of another New Yorker, their contemporary, Clement C. Moore.

The most of the American poets of a larger reputation have condescended to the lighter lyric upon occasion, and have written poems which fulfil the triple qualification of brevity, brilliancy, and buoyancy. Even the austere Bryant unbent his brows for once to tell in rhyme the tricksy habits of the bobolink; while Emerson chose rather to address himself with witty wisdom and glancing fantasy "To the Humble Bee." The grave and sedate Longfellow was willing to appear rather rollicking, in his swinging stanzas in praise of "Catawba-Wine"; and the simple Whittier once again went back to the years of his youth and in "School-Days" gave us a picture as clear as any of Prior's or Praed's and with a tenderness even more delicately suggested. This poem of Whittier's is evidence of the accuracy of Lowell's assertion that "sentiment is intellectualized emotion,—emotion precipitated, as it were, in pretty crystals by the fancy."

Lowell's own verse was too earnest and too strenuous for him often to be content with this sort of sentiment, which he called "the delightful staple of the poets of social life like Horace and Béranger.... It puts into words for us that decorous average of

INTRODUCTION

feeling to the expression of which society can consent without danger of being indiscreetly moved. . . . It is the sufficing lyrical interpreter of those lighter hours that should make part of every man's day. . . . True sentiment is emotion ripened by a slow ferment of the mind and qualified to an agreeable temperance by that taste which is the conscience of polite society." Had he so chosen Lowell might have been the master of all Americans who have attempted familiar verse. He seemed to have every qualification, — the ready humor, the good-tempered wit, and the sincere sentiment that never curdled into sentimentality. As it is, he has left us a half-a-dozen, or at the most, half-a-score of lyrics which belong by the side of the best examples of our social verse. "Without and Within" is perhaps the most widely known; and "Auf Wiedersehen" has been almost as popular.

It is Lowell's friend and fellow-professor that most critics would select as the foremost American songster of society; and this was also the opinion of Locker-Lampson, who declared in 1867 that Holmes was "perhaps the best living writer of this species of verse." Holmes's poems had most of them an eighteenth century flavor; and they might well have borne an eighteenth century title, "Poems on Several Occasions," since they had been so largely evoked by the current events in Boston, of which proud town he was the loyal bard. As he himself put it wittily,

> I 'm a florist in verse, and what would people say,
> If I came to a banquet without my bouquet?

Unfortunately these flowers of metrical rhetoric, which seem so fresh when first plucked, fade only too swiftly when the occasion has fallen out of memory; and it is not surprising that the most of Holmes's rhymes for events at once local and transient are now of lessening interest. But what is really astonishing is that so many of them have kept their vivacity as long as they have. Of Holmes's *vers de société* as distinguished from his *vers d'occasion*, the best are as bright now as ever they were. The "Last Leaf," for example, has not withered. In "Dorothy Q," again, in "Lending a Punch-Bowl," and in more than one other sprightly and sparkling lyric Holmes proves that society-verse may be, as Mr. Stedman has noted, "picturesque, even dramatic," and that it may "rise to a high degree of humor and of sage and tender thought." "Contentment" is another of Holmes's essays in familiar verse which is simply perfect in its ease and its certainty and its ironic humor. And the "Deacon's Masterpiece," — which most of us prefer to remember as the "One Hoss Shay," although perhaps a little too long and a little too satiric to be called *vers de société*, is one of the minor masterpieces of American literature.

Of the American poets who died before the nineteenth century drew to an end, three demand consideration here, — John Godfrey Saxe, Eugene Field, and Henry Cuyler Bunner. Of these Saxe was much the elder, by far the most old-fashioned in his method, and also the least individual. He had borrowed the knack of punning from Hood, and he had taken over the trick of antithesis from Praed. If Mr. Swinburne was right in asserting that even in the narrowest form of *vers de société*, we look "for more spirit and versatility of life, more warmth of touch, more fulness of tone, more vigor and variety of impulse than we find in Praed," — then it is hard for us to grant high rank to Saxe, who was little more than Praed once-removed. Sometimes Saxe skirts perilously close to vulgarity;

sometimes his humor is no better than crackling witticism; sometimes he fails to achieve the elevation of tone which even familiar verse ought ever to attain; sometimes he lacks even the suggestion of that sentiment which ought to sustain *vers de société*. But sometimes his success is evident and undeniable, as in the "Mourner à la Mode," for example, and in "Early Rising," and more especially in "Little Jerry," a perfect portrait deftly touched with tenderness.

Eugene Field resembled Saxe at least in one respect, — his broadly comic lyrics are more abundant than his social verse. His humor was so spontaneous that it often became almost acrobatic, revelling in the exuberance of its own fun. He delighted in the apt use of slang; and it is his indulgence in this fondness for vernacular freshness which must rule out the "Truth about Horace" from any careful anthology of social verse, in spite of its brilliancy and its buoyancy. Field had not only a deeper knowledge of literature than Saxe, he had also a wider outlook on life. He had more originality, a richer native gift of metrical expression, a keener ingenuity in handling both rhyme and rhythm, a more daring adroitness of epithet; above all, he had far more feeling, and his sentiment was sincerer and sturdier. Of a certainty "Little Boy Blue" is the most popular of Field's poems, — and it is also his finest effort in the limited field of familiar verse. "Thirty-nine" and "Old Times, Old Friends, Old Loves" have the same note of sentiment, more playful but not less pure. And even "Apple-Pie and Cheese," frolicsome as it is in its rhythm and in its gaiety, is still restrained enough and sufficiently decorous to come within the canon of *vers de société*. Indeed it is curious to note how often good things to eat and to drink have inspired the songsters of society; and Field's "Apple-Pie and Cheese" is the nineteenth century mate of Barlow's eighteenth century "Hasty-Pudding."

Bunner was more truly a poet than either Field or Saxe: he could strike a loftier note than they, at once more resonant and more appealing; his humor is more subtly united with his pathos; his lyre was more obviously a winged instrument than either of theirs. The "Way to Arcady" has a freedom, an easy lightness, a graceful gentleness, a simplicity of sentiment, rarely seen in combination nowadays, although not infrequent in the slighter songs of the Elizabethan dramatists. It was in fact the song of one who had skirted the coast of Bohemia on his way to the forest of Arden, where he was to feel himself at home, listening to the shepherds as they piped and looking on as the shepherdesses danced in the spring sunshine. Not only had Bunner profited by the example of Herrick and of Suckling, he had also felt the force of Heine's lyric irony and he had come under the charm of Mr. Austin Dobson's captivating music. His originality was compounded of many simples; but when he possessed it at last, it was all his own. "Forfeits" and "Candor" are absolutely within the narrowest definition of society-verse; and they have an indisputable individuality of their own. So has the "Chaperon," with its flavor of old-time tenderness. So has "One, Two, Three," with its exquisite certainty of touch and its artful escape from sentimentality.

Of the living it is always less easy to speak with all due restraint than it is to criticize calmly those who have gone before, leaving us only their writings to influence the pending decision. Yet it would be absurd to omit here all mention of two of the

INTRODUCTION

American masters of familiar verse, Mr. Edmund Clarence Stedman and Mr. Thomas Bailey Aldrich. Theirs is never society-verse in its narrower sense, for their lightest lyrics are always poetry, with no trace of the striving and with no taint of the cheap smartness which only too often contaminates mere society-verse. Rather is theirs familiar verse in its most refined perfection, such as Cowper would have relished. Mr. Aldrich's "Nocturne" has a spontaneity and a delicate grace that Herrick would have appreciated; and Mr. Stedman's "Pan in Wall Street" has a commingling of wit with sentiment that recalls forerunners as dissimilar as Prior and Theocritus.

Other living American poets there are not a few who have adventured now and again in verse of this sort, seemingly so easy and actually so hard. The strict rule adopted for all the volumes of this series forbids the inclusion of the lighter lyrics of any living writer born in the second half of the nineteenth century, and thus debars the Editor from the privilege of selecting from the verse of Mr. J. Whitcomb Riley, Mr. Frank Dempster Sherman, Mr. H. K. Vielé, and Miss Helen G. Cone, worthy followers of those whose contributions have been here considered. Those who shall hereafter attempt this species of poetry may be encouraged by the fact that although success must needs be infrequent, its reward is as certain to-day as it was nearly a score of centuries ago when Pliny was writing to Tuscus that "it is surprizing how much the mind is entertained and enlivened by these little poetical compositions, as they turn upon subjects of gallantry, satire, tenderness, politeness, and everything, in short, that concern life, and the affairs of the world."

BENJAMIN FRANKLIN
1706-1790

PAPER

SOME wit of old — such wits of old there were —
Whose hints show'd meaning, whose allusions care,
By one brave stroke to mark all human kind,
Call'd clear blank paper every infant mind;
Where still, as opening sense her dictates wrote,
Fair virtue put a seal, or vice a blot.

The thought was happy, pertinent, and true;
Methinks a genius might the plan pursue.
I (can you pardon my presumption?) I —
No wit, no genius, yet for once will try.

Various the papers various wants produce,
The wants of fashion, elegance, and use.
Men are as various; and if right I scan,
Each sort of *paper* represents some *man*.

Pray note the fop — half powder and half lace —
Nice as a band-box were his dwelling-place:
He's the *gilt paper*, which apart you store,
And lock from vulgar hands in the 'scrutoire.

Mechanics, servants, farmers, and so forth,
Are *copy-paper*, of inferior worth;
Less prized, more useful, for your desk decreed,
Free to all pens, and prompt at every need.

The wretch, whom avarice bids to pinch and spare,
Starve, cheat, and pilfer, to enrich an heir,
Is coarse *brown paper;* such as pedlars choose
To wrap up wares, which better men will use.

Take next the miser's contrast, who destroys
Health, fame, and fortune, in a round of joys.
Will any paper match him? Yes, throughout,
He's a true *sinking-paper,* past all doubt.

The retail politician's anxious thought
Deems *this* side always right, and *that* stark naught;
He foams with censure; with applause he raves —
A dupe to rumors, and a tool of knaves;
He'll want no type his weakness to proclaim,
While such a thing as *foolscap* has a name.

The hasty gentleman, whose blood runs high,
Who picks a quarrel, if you step awry,
Who can't a jest, or hint, or look endure:
What is he? What? *Touch-paper* to be sure.

What are our poets, take them as they fall,
Good, bad, rich, poor, much read, not read at all?
Them and their works in the same class you'll find;
They are the mere *waste-paper* of mankind.

Observe the maiden, innocently sweet,
She's fair *white-paper,* an unsullied sheet;
On which the happy man, whom fate ordains,
May write his *name,* and take her for his pains.

One instance more, and only one I'll bring;
'T is the *great man* who scorns a little thing,
Whose thoughts, whose deeds, whose maxims are his own,
Form'd on the feelings of his heart alone:
True genuine *royal-paper* is his breast:
Of all the kinds most precious, purest, best.

FRANCIS HOPKINSON
1737 – 1791

SONG

MY generous heart disdains
    The slave of love to be;
I scorn his servile chains,
    And boast my liberty.
        This whining
        And pining
And wasting with care,
Are not to my taste, be she ever so fair.

Shall a girl's capricious frown
Sink my noble spirits down?
Shall a face of white and red
Make me droop my silly head?
Shall I set me down and sigh
For an eye-brow, or an eye?
For a braided lock of hair,
Curse my fortune and despair?
    My generous heart disdains, etc.

Still uncertain is to-morrow,
Not quite certain is to-day —
Shall I waste my time in sorrow?
Shall I languish life away?
All because a cruel maid
Hath not love with love repaid?
    My generous heart disdains, etc.

ELIZABETH GRAEME FERGUSON
1739 – 1801

THE COUNTRY PARSON

How happy is the country parson's lot!
   Forgetting bishops, as by them forgot;
Tranquil of spirit, with an easy mind,
To all his vestry's votes he sits resigned:
Of manners gentle, and of temper even,
He jogs his flocks, with easy pace, to heaven.
In Greek and Latin, pious books he keeps;
And, while his clerk sings psalms, he — soundly sleeps.
His garden fronts the sun's sweet orient beams,
And fat church-wardens prompt his golden dreams.
The earliest fruit, in his fair orchard, blooms;
And cleanly pipes pour out tobacco's fumes.
From rustic bridegroom oft he takes the ring;
And hears the milkmaid plaintive ballads sing.
Back-gammon cheats whole winter nights away,
And Pilgrim's Progress helps a rainy day.

NATHANIEL EVANS

1742-1767

AN ODE (ATTEMPTED IN THE MANNER OF HORACE) TO MY INGENIOUS FRIEND, MR. THOMAS GODFREY

WHILE you, dear Tom, are forced to roam,
   In search of fortune, far from home,
O'er bogs, o'er seas, and mountains;
I, too, debarr'd the soft retreat
Of shady groves, and murmur sweet
   Of silver-prattling fountains,

Must mingle with the bustling throng,
And bear my load of cares along,
   Like any other sinner:
For, where's the ecstasy in this, —
To loiter in poetic bliss,
   And go without a dinner?

Flaccus, we know, immortal bard!
With mighty kings and statesmen fared,
   And lived in cheerful plenty:
But now, in these degenerate days,
The slight reward of empty praise,
   Scarce one receives in twenty.

Well might the Roman swan, along
The pleasing Tiber pour his song,
   When bless'd with ease and quiet;

Oft did he grace Maecenas' board,
Who would for him throw by the lord,
   And in Falernian riot.

But, dearest Tom! those days are past,
And we are in a climate cast
   Where few the muse can relish;
Where all the doctrine now that 's told,
Is that a shining heap of gold
   Alone can man embellish.

Then since 't is thus, my honest friend,
If you be wise, my strain attend,
   And counsel sage adhere to;
With me, henceforward, join the crowd,
And like the rest proclaim aloud,
   That money is all virtue!

Then may we both, in time, retreat
To some fair villa, sweetly neat,
   To entertain the muses;
And then life's noise and trouble leave —
Supremely blest, we 'll never grieve
   At what the world refuses.

PHILIP FRENEAU
1752 – 1832

THE PARTING GLASS

THE man that joins in life's career
   And hopes to find some comfort here,
To rise above this earthly mass, —
The only way 's to drink his glass.

But still, on this uncertain stage
Where hopes and fears the soul engage,
And while, amid the joyous band,
Unheeded flows the measured sand,
Forget not as the moments pass
That time shall bring the parting glass!

The nymph who boasts no borrowed charms,
Whose sprightly wit my fancy warms, —
What though she tends this country inn,
And mixes wine, and deals out gin?
With such a kind, obliging lass,
I sigh to take the parting glass.

With him who always talks of gain
(Dull Momus, of the plodding train),
The wretch who thrives by others' woes,
And carries grief where'er he goes, —
With people of this knavish class
The first is still my parting glass.

With those that drink before they dine,
With him that apes the grunting swine,
Who fills his page with low abuse,
And strives to act the gabbling goose
Turned out by fate to feed on grass —
Boy, give me quick, the parting glass.

The man whose friendship is sincere,
Who knows no guilt, and feels no fear, —
It would require a heart of brass
With him to take the parting glass.

With him who quaffs his pot of ale,
Who holds to all an even scale,
Who hates a knave in each disguise,
And fears him not — whate'er his size —
With him, well pleased my days to pass,
May heaven forbid the Parting Glass!

STANZAS

OCCASIONED BY THE RUINS OF A COUNTRY
INN UNROOFED AND BLOWN DOWN
IN A STORM

WHERE now these mingled ruins lie
    A temple once to Bacchus rose,
Beneath whose roof, aspiring high,
    Full many a guest forgot his woes.

No more this dome, by tempests torn,
    Affords a social safe retreat;
But ravens here, with eye forlorn,
    And clustering bats henceforth will meet.

The Priestess of this ruined shrine,
    Unable to survive the stroke,
Presents no more the ruddy wine, —
    Her glasses gone, her china broke.

The friendly Host, whose social hand
    Accosted strangers at the door,
Has left at length his wonted stand,
    And greets the weary guest no more.

Old creeping Time, that brings decay,
    Might yet have spared these mouldering walls,
Alike beneath whose potent sway
    A temple or a tavern falls.

Is this the place where mirth and joy,
    Coy nymphs, and sprightly lads were found?
Indeed! no more the nymphs are coy,
    No more the flowing bowls go round.

Is this the place where festive song
   Deceived the wintry hours away?
No more the swains the tune prolong,
   No more the maidens join the lay.

Is this the place where Nancy slept
   In downy beds of blue and green?
Dame Nature here no vigils kept,
   No cold unfeeling guards were seen.

'T is gone! — and Nancy tempts no more;
   Deep, unrelenting silence reigns;
Of all that pleased, that charmed before,
   The tottering chimney scarce remains.

Ye tyrant winds, whose ruffian blast
   Through doors and windows blew too strong,
And all the roof to ruin cast,
   The roof that sheltered us so long,

Your wrath appeased, I pray be kind
   If Mopsus should the dome renew,
That we again may quaff his wine,
   Again collect our jovial crew.

TO A CATY-DID

IN a branch of willow hid
Sings the evening Caty-did:
From the lofty locust bough
Feeding on a drop of dew,
In her suit of green arrayed
Hear her singing in the shade —
Caty-did, Caty-did, Caty-did!

While upon a leaf you tread,
Or repose your little head
On your sheet of shadows laid,
All the day you nothing said:
Half the night your cheery tongue
Revelled out its little song, —
Nothing else but Caty-did.

From your lodging on the leaf
Did you utter joy or grief?
Did you only mean to say,
I have had my summer's day,
And am passing, soon, away
To the grave of Caty-did:
Poor, unhappy Caty-did!

But you would have uttered more
Had you known of nature's power;
From the world when you retreat,
And a leaf's your winding sheet,
Long before your spirit fled,
Who can tell but nature said, —
Live again, my Caty-did!
Live, and chatter Caty-did.

Tell me, what did Caty do?
Did she mean to trouble you?
Why was Caty not forbid
To trouble little Caty-did?
Wrong, indeed, at you to fling,
Hurting no one while you sing, —
Caty-did! Caty-did! Caty-did!

Why continue to complain?
Caty tells me she again
Will not give you plague or pain;
Caty says you may be hid,
Caty will not go to bed
While you sing us Caty-did, —
Caty-did! Caty-did! Caty-did!

But, while singing, you forgot
To tell us what did Caty *not:*
Caty did not think of cold,
Flocks retiring to the fold,
Winter with his wrinkles old;
Winter, that yourself foretold
When you gave us Caty-did.

Stay serenely on your nest;
Caty now will do her best,
All she can, to make you blest;
But you want no human aid, —
Nature, when she formed you, said,
"Independent you are made,
My dear little Caty-did:
Soon yourself must disappear
With the verdure of the year,"
And to go, we know not where,
With your song of Caty-did.

ROYALL TYLER

1757 – 1826

MY MISTRESSES

LET Cowley soft in amorous verse
　The rovings of his love rehearse,
　　With passion most unruly,
Boast how he woo'd sweet Amoret,
The sobbing Jane, and sprightly Bet,
The lily fair and smart brunette,
　　In sweet succession truly.

But list, ye lovers, and you 'll swear,
I roved with him beyond compare,
　　And was far more unlucky.
For never yet in Yankee coast
Were found such girls, who so could boast,
An honest lover's heart to roast,
　　From Casco to Kentucky.

When first the girls nicknamed me beau,
And I was all for dress and show,
　　I set me out a courting.
A romping miss, with heedless art,
First caught, then almost broke, my heart.
Miss Conduct named; we soon did part,
　　I did not like such sporting.

The next coquette, who raised a flame,
Was far more grave, and somewhat lame,
   She in my heart did rankle.
She conquer'd, with a sudden glance:
The spiteful slut was call'd Miss Chance;
I took the gipsy out to dance;
   She almost broke my ankle.

A thoughtless girl, just in her teens,
   Was the next fair, whom love it seems
   Had made me prize most highly.
I thought to court a lovely mate,
But, how it made my heart to ache;
It was that jade, the vile Miss Take;
   In troth, love did it slyly.

And last Miss Fortune, whimpering came,
Cured me of love's tormenting flame,
   And all my beau pretences.
In widow's weeds, the prude appears;
See now — she drowns me with her tears,
With bony fist, now slaps my ears,
   And brings me to my senses.

THE BOOKWORM

WHO is that meagre, studious wight,
    Who sports the habit of our days,
And, in the reigning mode's despite,
    His antique coat and vest displays?

In whose gaunt form, from head to feet,
    The antiquarian's air we trace,
While Hebrew roots and ancient Greek
    Plot out the features of his face.

His critic eye is fixed with glee
    On a worm-eaten, smoke-dried page;
The time-worn paper seems to be
    The relic of some long-past age.

In sooth, it is the manuscript
    Of this poor, feeble verse of mine;
Which, in despite of taste and wit,
    Has straggled down to future time.

The bookworm's features scrawl a smile
    While gloating on the musty page;
As we admire some ruined pile
    Not for its worth, but for its age.

The sprawling letters, yellow text,
   The formal phrase, the bald, stiff style,
The spelling quaint, the line perplexed,
   Provoke his unaccustomed smile.

Like Kennicut he cites and quotes,
   On illustration clear intent,
And in the margin gravely notes
   A thousand meanings never meant.

SAMUEL LOW
1765 -?

TO A SEGAR

SWEET antidote to sorrow, toil and strife,
   Charm against discontent and wrinkled care.
Who knows thy power can never know despair;
Who knows thee not, one solace lacks of life:
When cares oppress, or when the busy day
Gives place to tranquil eve, a single puff
Can drive even want and lassitude away,
And give a mourner happiness enough.
From thee when curling clouds of incense rise,
They hide each evil that in prospect lies;
But when in evanescence fades thy smoke,
Ah! what, dear sedative, my cares shall smother?
If thou evaporate, the charm is broke,
Till I, departing taper, light another.

JOHN QUINCY ADAMS
1767 – 1848

TO SALLY

THE man in righteousness arrayed,
  A pure and blameless liver,
Needs not the keen Toledo blade,
  Nor venom-freighted quiver.
What though he wind his toilsome way
  O'er regions wild and weary —
Through Zara's burning desert stray,
  Or Asia's jungles dreary:

What though he plough the billowy deep
  By lunar light, or solar,
Meet the resistless Simoon's sweep,
  Or iceberg circumpolar!
In bog or quagmire deep and dank
  His foot shall never settle;
He mounts the summit of Mont Blanc,
  Or Popocatapetl.

On Chimborazo's breathless height
  He treads o'er burning lava;
Or snuffs the Bohan Upas blight,
  The deathful plant of Java.
Through every peril he shall pass,
  By Virtue's shield protected;
And still by Truth's unerring glass
  His path shall be directed.

Else wherefore was it, Thursday last,
  While strolling down the valley,
Defenceless, musing as I passed
  A canzonet to Sally,
A wolf, with mouth-protruding snout,
  Forth from the thicket bounded —
I clapped my hands and raised a shout —
  He heard — and fled — confounded.

Tangier nor Tunis never bred
  An animal more crabbed;
Nor Fez, dry-nurse of lions, fed
  A monster half so rabid;
Nor Ararat so fierce a beast
  Has seen since days of Noah;
Nor stronger, eager for a feast,
  The fell constrictor boa.

Oh! place me where the solar beam
  Has scorched all verdure vernal;
Or on the polar verge extreme,
  Blocked up with ice eternal —
Still shall my voice's tender lays
  Of love remain unbroken;
And still my charming Sally praise,
  Sweet smiling and sweet spoken.

WILLIAM MARTIN JOHNSON
1771 – 1797

ON SNOW-FLAKES MELTING ON HIS LADY'S BREAST

TO kiss my Celia's fairer breast,
   The snow forsakes its native skies,
But proving an unwelcome guest,
   It grieves, dissolves in tears, and dies.

Its touch, like mine, but serves to wake
   Through all her frame a death-like chill, —
Its tears, like those I shed, to make
   That icy bosom colder still.

I blame her not; from Celia's eyes
   A common fate beholders prove —
Each swain, each fair one, weeps and dies, —
   With envy these, and those with love!

JOHN SHAW
1778 – 1809

SONG

WHO has robbed the ocean cave,
    To tinge thy lips with coral hue?
Who from India's distant wave
    For thee those pearly treasures drew?
        Who, from yonder orient sky,
        Stole the morning of thine eye?

Thousand charms, thy form to deck,
    From sea, and earth, and air are torn;
Roses bloom upon thy cheek,
    On thy breath their fragrance borne.
        Guard thy bosom from the day,
        Lest thy snows should melt away.

But one charm remains behind,
    Which mute earth can ne'er impart;
Nor in ocean wilt thou find,
    Nor in the circling air, a heart.
        Fairest! wouldst thou perfect be,
        Take, oh take that heart from me.

CLEMENT CLARKE MOORE
1779 – 1863

A VISIT FROM ST. NICHOLAS

'TWAS the night before Christmas, when all through the house
Not a creature was stirring, not even a mouse;
The stockings were hung by the chimney with care,
In hopes that St. NICHOLAS soon would be there;
The children were nestled all snug in their beds,
While visions of sugar-plums danced in their heads;
And mamma in her 'kerchief, and I in my cap,
Had just settled our brains for a long winter's nap,
When out on the lawn there arose such a clatter,
I sprang from the bed to see what was the matter.
Away to the window I flew like a flash,
Tore open the shutters and threw up the sash.
The moon on the breast of the new-fallen snow
Gave the lustre of mid-day to objects below,
When, what to my wondering eyes should appear,
But a miniature sleigh, and eight tiny reindeer,
With a little old driver, so lively and quick,
I knew in a moment it must be St. Nick.
More rapid than eagles his coursers they came,
And he whistled, and shouted, and called them by name;
"Now, *Dasher!* now, *Dancer!* now, *Prancer* and *Vixen!*
On, *Comet!* on, *Cupid!* on, *Donder* and *Blitzen!*
To the top of the porch! to the top of the wall!
Now dash away! dash away! dash away all!"

As dry leaves that before the wild hurricane fly,
When they meet with an obstacle, mount to the sky;
So up to the house-top the coursers they flew,
With the sleigh full of Toys, and St. Nicholas too.
And then, in a twinkling, I heard on the roof
The prancing and pawing of each little hoof.
As I drew in my head, and was turning around,
Down the chimney St. Nicholas came with a bound.
He was dressed all in fur, from his head to his foot,
And his clothes were all tarnished with ashes and soot;
A bundle of Toys he had flung on his back,
And he looked like a pedler just opening his pack.
His eyes — how they twinkled! his dimples how merry!
His cheeks were like roses, his nose like a cherry!
His droll little mouth was drawn up like a bow,
And the beard of his chin was as white as the snow;
The stump of a pipe he held tight in his teeth,
And the smoke it encircled his head like a wreath;
He had a broad face and a little round belly,
That shook when he laughed, like a bowlful of jelly.
He was chubby and plump, a right jolly old elf,
And I laughed when I saw him, in spite of myself;
A wink of his eye and a twist of his head,
Soon gave me to know I had nothing to dread;
He spoke not a word, but went straight to his work,
And filled all the stockings; then turned with a jerk,
And laying his finger aside of his nose,
And giving a nod, up the chimney he rose;
He sprang to his sleigh, to his team gave a whistle,
And away they all flew like the down of a thistle.
But I heard him exclaim, ere he drove out of sight,
"*Happy Christmas to all, and to all a good-night.*"

JAMES KIRKE PAULDING
1779 – 1860

THE OLD MAN'S CAROUSAL

DRINK! drink! to whom shall we drink?
To a friend or a mistress? Come, let me think!
To those who are absent, or those who are here?
To the dead that we loved, or the living still dear?
Alas! when I look, I find none of the last!
The present is barren, — let's drink to the past!

Come! here's to the girl with a voice sweet and low,
The eye all of fire and the bosom of snow,
Who erewhile, in the days of my youth that are fled,
Once slept on my bosom, and pillowed my head!
Would you know where to find such a delicate prize?
Go seek in yon church-yard, for there she lies.

And here's to the friend, the one friend of my youth,
With a head full of genius, a heart full of truth,
Who travelled with me in the sunshine of life,
And stood by my side in its peace and its strife!
Would you know where to seek for a blessing so rare?
Go drag the lone sea, you may find him there.

And here's to a brace of twin cherubs of mine,
With hearts like their mother's, as pure as this wine,
Who came but to see the first act of the play,
Grew tired of the scene, and then both went away.

Would you know where this brace of bright cherubs have hied?
Go seek them in heaven, for there they abide.

A bumper, my boys! to a gray-headed pair,
Who watched o'er my childhood with tenderest care.
God bless them, and keep them, and may they look down
On the head of their son, without tear, sigh, or frown!
Would you know whom I drink to? go seek 'mid the dead,
You will find both their names on the stone at their head.

And here's — but alas! the good wine is no more,
The bottle is emptied of all its bright store;
Like those we have toasted, its spirit is fled,
And nothing is left of the light that it shed.
Then, a bumper of tears, boys! the banquet here ends.
With a health to our dead, since we've no living friends.

WASHINGTON IRVING
1783 – 1859

ALBUM VERSES

THOU record of the votive throng,
    That fondly seek this fairy shrine,
And pay the tribute of a song
    Where worth and loveliness combine, —

What boots that I, a vagrant wight
    From clime to clime still wandering on,
Upon thy friendly page should write
    — Who 'll think of me when I am gone?

Go plough the wave, and sow the sand!
    Throw seed to ev'ry wind that blows;
Along the highway strew thy hand,
    And fatten on the crop that grows.

For even thus the man that roams
    On heedless hearts his feeling spends;
Strange tenant of a thousand homes,
    And friendless, with ten thousand friends!

WASHINGTON IRVING

Yet here, for once, I'll leave a trace,
   To ask in after times a thought!
To say that here a resting-place
   My wayworn heart has fondly sought.

So the poor pilgrim heedless strays,
   Unmoved, thro' many a region fair;
But at some shrine his tribute pays
   To tell that he has worshipp'd there.

A CERTAIN YOUNG LADY

THERE'S a certain young lady,
    Who's just in her heyday,
And full of all mischief, I ween;
    So teasing! so pleasing!
    Capricious! delicious!
And you know very well whom I mean.

With an eye dark as night,
Yet than noonday more bright,
    Was ever a black eye so keen?
    It can thrill with a glance,
    With a beam can entrance,
And you know very well whom I mean.

With a stately step — such as
You'd expect in a duchess —
    And a brow might distinguish a queen,
    With a mighty proud air,
    That says "touch me who dare,"
And you know very well whom I mean.

With a toss of the head
That strikes one quite dead,
    But a smile to revive one again;
    That toss so appalling!
    That smile so enthralling!
And you know very well whom I mean.

Confound her! devil take her! —
A cruel heart-breaker —
   But hold! see that smile so serene.
     God love her! God bless her!
     May nothing distress her!
   You know very well whom I mean.

Heaven help the adorer
Who happens to bore her,
   The lover who wakens her spleen;
     But too blest for a sinner
     Is he who shall win her,
   And you know very well whom I mean.

WILLIAM MAXWELL
1784–1857

TO A FAIR LADY

FAIREST, mourn not for thy charms,
  Circled by no lover's arms,
While inferior belles you see
Pick up husbands merrily.
Sparrows, when they choose to pair,
Meet their matches anywhere;
But the Phoenix, sadly great,
Cannot find an equal mate.
Earth, tho' dark, enjoys the honor
Of a moon to wait upon her;
Venus, tho' divinely bright,
Cannot boast a satellite.

TO ANNE

How many kisses do I ask?
Now you set me to my task.
First, sweet Anne, will you tell me
How many waves are in the sea?
How many stars are in the sky?
How many lovers you make sigh?
How many sands are on the shore?
I shall want just one kiss more.

WILLIAM CULLEN BRYANT
1794 – 1878

ROBERT OF LINCOLN

MERRILY swinging on brier and weed,
  Near to the nest of his little dame,
Over the mountain-side or mead,
  Robert of Lincoln is telling his name:
    Bob-o'-link, bob-o'-link,
    Spink, spank, spink;
Snug and safe is that nest of ours,
Hidden among the summer flowers.
          Chee, chee, chee.

Robert of Lincoln is gayly drest,
  Wearing a bright black wedding coat;
White are his shoulders and white his crest,
  Here him call in his merry note:
    Bob-o'-link, bob-o'-link,
    Spink, spank, spink;
Look, what a nice new coat is mine,
Sure there was never a bird so fine.
          Choo, choo, choo.

Robert of Lincoln's Quaker wife,
  Pretty and quiet, with plain brown wings,
Passing at home a patient life,
  Broods in the grass while her husband sings:

Bob-o'-link, bob-o'-link,
  Spink, spank, spink;
Brood, kind creature; you need not fear
Thieves and robbers while I am here.
        Chee, chee, chee.

Modest and shy as a nun is she;
  One weak chirp is her only note.
Braggart and prince of braggarts is he,
  Pouring boasts from his little throat:
    Bob-o'-link, bob-o'-link,
    Spink, spank, spink;
Never was I afraid of man;
Catch me, cowardly knaves, if you can.
        Chee, chee, chee.

Six white eggs on a bed of hay,
  Flecked with purple, a pretty sight!
  There as the mother sits all day,
  Robert is singing with all his might:
    Bob-o' link, bob-o'-link,
    Spink, spank, spink;
Nice good wife, that never goes out,
Keeping house while I frolic about.
        Chee, chee, chee.

Soon as the little ones chip the shell
  Six wide mouths are open for food.
Robert of Lincoln bestirs him well,
  Gathering seeds for the hungry brood.
    Bob-o'-link, bob-o'-link,
    Spink, spank, spink;
This new life is likely to be
Hard for a gay young fellow like me.
        Chee, chee, chee.

Robert of Lincoln at length is made
   Sober with work, and silent with care;
Off is his holiday garment laid,
   Half forgotten that merry air,
      Bob-o'-link, bob-o'-link,
      Spink, spank, spink;
Nobody knows but my mate and I
Where our nest and our nestlings lie.
          Chee, chee, chee.

Summer wanes; the children are grown;
   Fun and frolic no more he knows;
Robert of Lincoln's a humdrum crone;
   Off he flies, and we sing as he goes:
      Bob-o'-link, bob-o'-link,
      Spink, spank, spink;
When you can pipe that merry old strain,
Robert of Lincoln, come back again.
          Chee, chee, chee.

FITZGREENE HALLECK
1790 – 1867

ODE TO FORTUNE

[*In collaboration with Joseph Rodman Drake*]

FAIR lady with the bandaged eye!
   I 'll pardon all thy scurvy tricks,
So thou wilt cut me, and deny
   Alike thy kisses and thy kicks:
I 'm quite contented as I am,
   Have cash to keep my duns at bay,
Can choose between beefsteaks and ham,
   And drink Madeira every day.

My station is the middle rank,
   My fortune — just a competence —
Ten thousand in the Franklin Bank,
   And twenty in the six per cents;
No amorous chains my heart enthrall,
   I neither borrow, lend, nor sell;
Fearless I roam the City Hall,
   And bite my thumb at Sheriff Bell.

The horse that twice a week I ride
   At Mother Dawson's eats his fill;
My books at Goodrich's abide,
   My country-seat is Weehawk hill;

My morning lounge is Eastburn's shop,
   At Poppleton's I take my lunch,
Niblo prepares my mutton-chop,
   And Jennings makes my whiskey-punch.

When merry, I the hours amuse
   By squibbing Bucktails, Guards, and Balls,
And when I'm troubled with the blues
   Damn Clinton and abuse canals :
Then, Fortune, since I ask no prize,
   At least preserve me from thy frown !
The man who don't attempt to rise
   'T were cruelty to tumble down.

WOMAN

[*Written in the album of an unknown lady*]

LADY, although we have not met,
   And may not meet, beneath the sky;
And whether thine are eyes of jet,
Gray, or dark blue, or violet,
   Or hazel — Heaven knows, not I;

Whether around thy cheek of rose
   A maiden's glowing locks are curled,
And to some thousand kneeling beaux
Thy frown is cold as winter's snows,
   Thy smile is worth a world;

Or whether, past youth's joyous strife,
   The calm of thought is on thy brow,
And thou art in thy noon of life,
Loving and loved, a happy wife,
   And happier mother now —

I know not: but, whate'er thou art,
   Whoe'er thou art, were mine the spell,
To call Fate's joys or blunt his dart,
There should not be one hand or heart
   But served or wished thee well.

For thou art woman — with that word
   Life's dearest hopes and memories come
Truth, Beauty, Love — in her adored,
And earth's lost Paradise restored
   In the green bower of home.

What is man's love?   His vows are broke,
　　Even while his parting kiss is warm;
But woman's love all change will mock,
And, like the ivy round the oak,
　　Cling closest in the storm.

And well the Poet at her shrine
　　May bend, and worship while he woos;
To him she is a thing divine,
The inspiration of his line,
　　His Sweetheart and his Muse.

If to his song the echo rings
　　Of Fame — 't is woman's voice he hears;
If ever from his lyre's proud strings
Flow sounds like rush of angel-wings,
'T is that she listens while he sings,
　　With blended smiles and tears:

Smiles — tears — whose blessed and blessing power,
　　Like sun and dew o'er summer's tree,
Alone keeps green through Time's long hour,
That frailer thing than leaf or flower,
　　A poet's immortality.

JOSEPH RODMAN DRAKE
1795 – 1820

THE MAN WHO FRETS AT WORLDLY STRIFE

THE man who frets at worldly strife
   Grows sallow, sour, and thin;
Give us the lad whose happy life
   Is one perpetual grin:
He, Midas-like, turns all to gold, —
   He smiles when others sigh,
Enjoys alike the hot and cold,
   And laughs through wet and dry.

There's fun in everything we meet, —
   The greatest, worst, and best;
Existence is a merry treat,
   And every speech a jest:
Be 't ours to watch the crowds that pass
   Where Mirth's gay banner waves;
To show fools through a quizzing-glass,
   And bastinade the knaves.

The serious world will scold and ban,
   In clamor loud and hard,
To hear Meigs called a Congressman,
   And Paulding styled a bard;
But, come what may, the man's in luck
   Who turns it all to glee,
And laughing, cries, with honest Puck,
   "Good Lord! what fools ye be."

INCONSTANCY

YES! I swore to be true, I allow,
   And I meant it, but, some how or other,
The seal of that amorous vow
   Was pressed on the lips of another.

Yet I did but as all would have done,
   For where is the being, dear cousin,
Content with the beauties of one
   When he might have the range of a dozen?

Young Love is a changeable boy,
   And the gem of the sea-rock is like him,
For he gives back the beams of his joy
   To each sunny eye that may strike him.

From a kiss of a zephyr and rose
   Love sprang in an exquisite hour,
And fleeting and sweet, heaven knows,
   Is this child of a sigh and a flower.

TO A LADY

WHO DECLARED THAT THE SUN PREVENTED HER FROM SLEEPING

WHY blame old Sol, who, all on fire,
   Prints on your lip the burning kiss;
Why should he not your charms admire,
   And dip his beam each morn in bliss?

Were 't mine to guide o'er paths of light
   The beam-haired coursers of the sky,
I 'd stay their course the livelong night
   To gaze upon thy sleeping eye.

Then let the dotard fondly spring,
   Each rising day, to snatch the prize;
'T will add new vigour to his wing,
   And speed his journey through the skies.

EDWARD COATE PINKNEY

1802 – 1828

A HEALTH

I FILL this cup to one made up
   Of loveliness alone —
A woman of her gentle sex
   The seeming paragon!
To whom the better elements
   And kindly stars have given
A form so fair, that like the air,
   'T is less of earth than heaven.

Her every tone is music's own,
   Like those of morning birds,
And something more than melody
   Dwells ever in her words.
The coinage of her heart are they,
   And from her lip each flows
As one may see the burthened bee
   Forth issue from the rose!

Affections are as thoughts to her,
   The measure of her hours;
Her feelings have the fragrancy,
   The freshness of young flowers!
While lovely passions changing oft,
   So fill her, she appears
By turns the image of themselves —
   The idol of past years.

Of her bright face, one glance will trace
   A picture on the brain;
And of her voice in echoing hearts
   A sound must long remain;
But memory, such as mine of her,
   So very much endears,
When death is nigh, my latest sigh,
   Will not be life's, but hers.

I fill this cup to one made up
   Of loveliness alone —
A woman of her gentle sex
   The seeming paragon!
Her health! and would on earth there stood
   Some more of such a frame!
That life might be all poetry,
   And weariness a name.

ALBERT GORTON GREENE
1802 – 1868

OLD GRIMES

OLD Grimes is dead; that good old man
    We never shall see more:
He used to wear a long, black coat,
    All buttoned down before.

His heart was open as the day,
    His feelings all were true;
His hair was some inclined to gray —
    He wore it in a queue.

Whene'er he heard the voice of pain,
    His breast with pity burn'd;
The large, round head upon his cane
    From ivory was turn'd.

Kind words he ever had for all;
    He knew no base design:
His eyes were dark and rather small,
    His nose was aquiline.

He lived at peace with all mankind,
    In friendship he was true:
His coat had pocket-holes behind,
    His pantaloons were blue.

ALBERT GORTON GREENE

Unharm'd, the sin which earth pollutes
    He pass'd securely o'er,
And never wore a pair of boots
    For thirty years or more.

But good old Grimes is now at rest,
    Nor fears misfortune's frown:
He wore a double-breasted vest —
    The stripes ran up and down.

He modest merit sought to find,
    And pay it its desert:
He had no malice in his mind,
    No ruffles on his shirt.

His neighbors he did not abuse —
    Was sociable and gay:
He wore large buckles on his shoes
    And changed them every day.

His knowledge, hid from public gaze,
    He did not bring to view,
Nor made a noise, town-meeting days,
    As many people do.

His worldly goods he never threw
    In trust to fortune's chances,
But lived (as all his brothers do)
    In easy circumstances.

Thus undisturb'd by anxious cares,
    His peaceful moments ran;
And everybody said he was
    A fine old gentleman.

RALPH WALDO EMERSON
1803 - 1882

THE HUMBLE-BEE

BURLY, dozing humble-bee,
Where thou art is clime for me.
Let them sail for Porto Rique,
Far-off heats through seas to seek;
I will follow thee alone,
Thou animated torrid-zone!
Zigzag steerer, desert cheerer,
Let me chase thy waving lines;
Keep me nearer, me thy hearer,
Singing over shrubs and vines.

Insect lover of the sun,
Joy of thy dominion!
Sailor of the atmosphere;
Swimmer through the waves of air;
Voyager of light and noon;
Epicurean of June;
Wait, I prithee, till I come
Within earshot of thy hum, —
All without is martyrdom.

When the south wind, in May days,
With a net of shining haze
Silvers the horizon wall,
And with softness touching all,

Tints the human countenance
With the color of romance,
And infusing subtle heats,
Turns the sod to violets,
Thou, in sunny solitudes,
Rover of the underwoods,
The green silence dost displace
With thy mellow, breezy bass.

Hot midsummer's petted crone,
Sweet to me thy drowsy tone
Tells of countless sunny hours,
Long days, and solid banks of flowers;
Of gulfs of sweetness without bound
In Indian wildernesses found;
Of Syrian peace, immortal leisure,
Firmest cheer, and bird-like pleasure.

Aught unsavory or unclean
Hath my insect never seen;
But violets and bilberry bells,
Maple-sap and daffodels,
Grass with green flag half-mast high,
Succory to match the sky,
Columbine with horn of honey,
Scented fern and agrimony,
Clover, catchfly, adder's-tongue
And brier-roses, dwelt among;
All beside was unknown waste,
All was picture as he passed.

Wiser far than human seer,
Yellow-breeched philosopher
Seeing only what is fair,
Sipping only what is sweet,
Thou dost mock at fate and care,
Leave the chaff and take the wheat.

When the fierce northwestern blast
Cools sea and land so far and fast,
Thou already slumberest deep;
Woe and want thou canst outsleep;
Want and woe, which torture us,
Thy sleep makes ridiculous.

NATHANIEL PARKER WILLIS
1806 – 1867

LOVE IN A COTTAGE

THEY may talk of love in a cottage,
    And bowers of trelised vine —
Of nature bewitchingly simple,
    And milkmaids half divine;
They may talk of the pleasures of sleeping
    In the shade of a spreading tree,
And a walk in the fields at morning,
    By the side of a footstep free!

But give me a sly flirtation
    By the light of a chandelier —
With music to play in the pauses,
    And nobody very near;
Or a seat on a silken sofa,
    With a glass of pure old wine,
And mamma too blind to discover
    The small white hand in mine.

Your love in a cottage is hungry,
    Your vine is a nest for flies —
Your milkmaid shocks the Graces,
    And simplicity talks of pies!
You lie down to your shady slumber
    And wake with a bug in your ear,
And your damsel that walks in the morning
    Is shod like a mountaineer.

True love is at home on a carpet,
   And mightily likes his ease —
And true love has an eye for a dinner,
   And starves beneath shady trees.
His wing is the fan of a lady,
   His foot's an invisible thing,
And his arrow is tipp'd with a jew
   And shot from a silver string.

CHARLES FENNO HOFFMAN
1806 – 1884

SPARKLING AND BRIGHT

SPARKLING and bright in liquid light,
  Does the wine our goblets gleam in,
With hue as red as the rosy bed
  Which a bee would choose to dream in.
    *Then fill to-night, with hearts as light,
      To loves as gay and fleeting
    As bubbles that swim on the beaker's brim,
      And break on the lips while meeting.*

Oh! if Mirth might arrest the flight
  Of Time through Life's dominions,
We here a while would now beguile
  The graybeard of his pinions,
    *To drink to-night, with hearts as light,
      To love as gay and fleeting
    As bubbles that swim on the beaker's brim,
      And break on the lips while meeting.*

But since Delight can't tempt the wight
  Nor fond Regret delay him,
Nor Love himself can hold the elf,
  Nor sober Friendship stay him,
    *We'll drink to-night, with hearts as light,
      To loves as gay and fleeting
    As bubbles that swim on the beaker's brim,
      And break on lips while meeting.*

ROSALIE CLARE

WHO owns not she's peerless — calls her not fair —
  Who questions the beauty of Rosalie Clare?
Let him saddle his courser and spur to the field,
And though coated in proof, he must perish or yield;
For no gallant can splinter — no charger can dare
The lance that is couched for young Rosalie Clare.

When goblets are flowing, and wit at the board
Sparkles high, while the blood of the red grape is poured,
And fond wishes for fair ones around offered up
From each lip that is wet with the dew of the cup, —
What name on the brimmer floats oftener there,
Or is whispered more warmly, than Rosalie Clare?

They may talk of the land of the olive and vine —
Of the maids of the Ebro, the Arno, or Rhine; —
Of the Houris that gladden the East with their smiles,
Where the sea's studded over with green summer isles;
But what flower of far away clime can compare
With the blossom of ours — bright Rosalie Clare?

Who owns not she's peerless — who calls her not fair?
Let him meet but the glances of Rosalie Clare!
Let him list to her voice — let him gaze on her form —
And if, hearing and seeing, his soul do not warm,
Let him go breathe it out in some less happy air
Than that which is blessed by sweet Rosalie Clare.

JOHN GREENLEAF WHITTIER
1807 – 1892

IN SCHOOL-DAYS

STILL sits the school-house by the road,
    A ragged beggar sunning;
Around it still the sumachs grow,
    And blackberry vines are running.

Within, the master's desk is seen,
    Deep scarred by raps official;
The warping floor, the battered seats,
    The jack-knife's carved initial;

The charcoal frescos on its wall;
    Its door's worn sill, betraying
The feet that, creeping slow to school,
    Went storming out to playing!

Long years ago a winter sun
    Shone over it at setting;
Lit up its western window-panes,
    And low eaves' icy fretting.

It touched the tangled golden curls,
    And brown eyes full of grieving,
Of one who still her steps delayed
    When all the school were leaving.

For near her stood the little boy
  Her childish favor singled :
His cap pulled low upon a face
  Where pride and shame were mingled.

Pushing with restless feet the snow
  To right and left, he lingered ; —
As restlessly her tiny hands
  The blue-checked apron fingered.

He saw her lift her eyes; he felt
  The soft hand's light caressing,
And heard the tremble of her voice.
  As if a fault confessing.

" I 'm sorry that I spelt the word :
  I hate to go above you,
Because," — the brown eyes lower fell —
  " Because, you see, I love you ! "

Still memory to a gray-haired man
  That sweet child-face is showing.
Dear girl! the grasses on her grave
  Have forty years been growing !

He lives to learn, in life's hard school,
  How few who pass above him
Lament their triumph and his loss,
  Like her, — because they love him.

THE BAREFOOT BOY

BLESSINGS on thee, little man,
Barefoot boy, with cheek of tan!
With thy turned-up pantaloons,
And thy merry whistled tunes;
With thy red lip, redder still
Kissed by strawberries on the hill;
With the sunshine on thy face,
Through thy torn brim's jaunty grace;
From my heart I give thee joy, —
I was once a barefoot boy!
Prince thou art, — the grown-up man
Only is republican.
Let the million-dollared ride!
Barefoot, trudging at his side,
Thou hast more than he can buy
In the reach of ear and eye, —
Outward sunshine, inward joy:
Blessings on thee, barefoot boy!

Oh for boyhood's painless play,
Sleep that wakes in laughing day,
Health that mocks the doctor's rules,
Knowledge never learned of schools,
Of the wild bee's morning chase,
Of the wild-flower's time and place,
Flight of fowl and habitude
Of the tenants of the wood;

How the tortoise bears his shell,
How the woodchuck digs his cell,
And the ground-mole sinks his well;
How the robin feeds her young,
How the oriole's nest is hung;
Where the whitest lilies blow,
Where the freshest berries grow,
Where the ground-nut trails its vine,
Where the wood-grape's clusters shine;
Of the black wasp's cunning way,
Mason of his walls of clay,
And the architectural plans
Of gray hornet artisans!
For, eschewing books and tasks,
Nature answers all he asks;
Hand in hand with her he walks,
Face to face with her he talks,
Part and parcel of her joy, —
Blessings on the barefoot boy!

Oh for boyhood's time of June,
Crowding years in one brief moon,
When all things I heard or saw,
Me, their master, waited for.
I was rich in flowers and trees,
Humming-birds and honey-bees;
For my sport the squirrel played,
Plied the snouted mole his spade;
For my taste the blackberry cone
Purpled over hedge and stone;
Laughed the brook for my delight
Through the day and through the night,
Whispering at the garden wall,
Talked with me from fall to fall;
Mine the sand-rimmed pickerel pond,
Mine the walnut slopes beyond,

Mine, on bending orchard trees,
Apples of Hesperides!
Still as my horizon grew,
Larger grew my riches too;
All the world I saw or knew
Seemed a complex Chinese toy,
Fashioned for a barefoot boy!

Oh for festal dainties spread,
Like my bowl of milk and bread;
Pewter spoon and bowl of wood,
On the door-stone, gray and rude!
O'er me, like a regal tent,
Cloudy-ribbed, the sunset bent,
Purple-curtained, fringed with gold,
Looped in many a wind-swung fold;
While for music came the play
Of the pied frogs' orchestra;
And, to light the noisy choir,
Lit the fly his lamp of fire.
I was monarch: pomp and joy
Waited on the barefoot boy!

Cheerily, then, my little man,
Live and laugh, as boyhood can!
Though the flinty slopes be hard,
Stubble-speared the new-mown sward,
Every morn shall lead thee through
Fresh baptisms of the dew;
Every evening from thy feet
Shall the cool wind kiss the heat:
All too soon these feet must hide
In the prison cells of pride,
Lose the freedom of the sod,
Like a colt's for work be shod,
Made to tread the mills of toil,
Up and down in ceaseless moil:

Happy if their track be found
Never on forbidden ground;
Happy if they sink not in
Quick and treacherous sands of sin.
Ah! that thou couldst know thy joy,
Ere it passes, barefoot boy!

THE HENCHMAN

MY lady walks her morning round,
  My lady's page her fleet greyhound,
My lady's hair the fond winds stir,
And all the birds make songs for her.

Her thrushes sing in Rathburn bowers,
And Rathburn side is gay with flowers;
But ne'er like hers, in flower or bird,
Was beauty seen or music heard.

The distance of the stars is hers;
The least of all her worshippers,
The dust beneath her dainty heel,
She knows not that I see or feel.

Oh, proud and calm! — she cannot know
Where'er she goes with her I go;
Oh, cold and fair! — she cannot guess
I kneel to share her hound's caress!

Gay knights beside her hunt and hawk,
I rob their ears of her sweet talk;
Her suitors come from east and west,
I steal her smiles from every guest.

Unheard of her, in loving words,
I greet her with the song of birds;
I reach her with her green-armed bowers,
I kiss her with the lips of flowers.

The hound and I are on her trail,
The wind and I uplift her veil;
As if the calm, cold moon she were,
And I the tide, I follow her.

As unrebuked as they, I share
The license of the sun and air,
And in a common homage hide
My worship from her scorn and pride.

World-wide apart, and yet so near,
I breathe her charmèd atmosphere,
Wherein to her my service brings
The reverence due to holy things.

Her maiden pride, her haughty name,
My dumb devotion shall not shame;
The love that no return doth crave
To knightly levels lifts the slave.

No lance have I, in joust or fight,
To splinter in my lady's sight;
But, at her feet, how blest were I
For any need of hers to die!

HENRY WADSWORTH LONGFELLOW
1807 – 1882

CATAWBA WINE

THIS song of mine
 Is a Song of the Vine,
To be sung by the glowing embers
 Of wayside inns,
 When the rain begins
To darken the drear Novembers.

It is not a song
 Of the Scuppernong,
From warm Carolinian valleys,
 Nor the Isabel
 And the Muscadel
That bask in our garden alleys.

Nor the red Mustang,
 Whose clusters hang
O'er the waves of the Colorado,
 And the fiery flood
 Of whose purple blood
Has a dash of Spanish bravado.

For richest and best
Is the wine of the West,

That grows by the Beautiful River;
    Whose sweet perfume
    Fills all the room
With a benison on the giver.

    And as hollow trees
    Are the haunts of bees,
Forever going and coming;
    So this crystal hive
    Is all alive
With a swarming and buzzing and humming.

    Very good in its way
    Is the Verzenay,
Or the Sillery soft and creamy;
    But Catawba wine
    Has a taste more divine,
More dulcet, delicious, and dreamy.

    There grows no vine
    By the haunted Rhine,
By Danube or Guadalquiver,
    Nor on island or cape,
    That bears such a grape
As grows by the Beautiful River.

    Drugged is their juice
    For foreign use,
hen shipped o'er the reeling Atlantic,
    To rack our brains
    With the fever pains,
That have driven the Old World frantic.

    To the sewers and sinks
    With all such drinks,
And after them tumble the mixer;
    For a poison malign
    Is such Borgia's wine,
Or at best but a Devil's Elixir.

While pure as a spring
Is the wine I sing,
And to praise it, one needs but name it;
For Catawba wine
Has need of no sign,
No tavern-bush to proclaim it.

And this Song of the Vine,
This greeting of mine,
The winds and the birds shall deliver
To the Queen of the West,
In her garlands dressed,
On the banks of the Beautiful River.

A DUTCH PICTURE

SIMON DANZ has come home again,
　　From cruising about with his buccaneers;
He has singed the beard of the King of Spain,
And carried away the Dean of Jaen
　　And sold him in Algiers.

In his house by the Maese, with its roof of tiles,
　　And weathercocks flying aloft in air,
There are silver tankards of antique styles,
Plunder of convent and castle, and piles
　　Of carpets rich and rare.

In his tulip-garden there by the town,
　　Overlooking the sluggish stream,
With his Moorish cap and dressing-gown,
The old sea-captain, hale and brown,
　　Walks in a waking dream.

A smile in his gray mustachio lurks
　　Whenever he thinks of the King of Spain;
And the listed tulips look like Turks,
And the silent gardener as he works
　　Is changed to the Dean of Jaen.

The windmills on the outermost
　　Verge of the landscape in the haze,
To him are towers on the Spanish coast,
With whiskered sentinels at their post,
　　Though this is the river Maese.

But when the winter rains begin,
    He sits and smokes by the blazing brands,
And old seafaring men come in,
Goat-bearded, gray, and with double chin,
    And rings upon their hands.

They sit there in the shadow and shine
    Of the flickering fire of the winter night;
Figures in color and design
Like those by Rembrandt of the Rhine,
    Half darkness and half light.

And they talk of ventures lost or won,
    And their talk is ever and ever the same,
While they drink the red wine of Tarragon,
From the cellars of some Spanish Don,
    Or convent set on flame.

Restless at times with heavy strides
    He paces his parlor to and fro;
He is like a ship that at anchor rides,
And swings with the rising and falling tides,
    And tugs at her anchor-tow.

Voices mysterious far and near,
    Sound of the wind and sound of the sea,
Are calling and whispering in his ear,
"Simon Danz! Why stayest thou here?
    Come forth and follow me!"

So he thinks he shall take to the sea again
    For one more cruise with his buccaneers,
To singe the beard of the King of Spain,
And capture another Dean of Jaen
    And sell him in Algiers.

BEWARE!

I KNOW a maiden fair to see,
    Take care!
She can both false and friendly be,
    Beware! Beware!
    Trust her not,
She is fooling thee!

She has two eyes, so soft and brown,
    Take care!
She gives a side-glance and looks down,
    Beware! Beware!
    Trust her not,
She is fooling thee!

And she has hair of a golden hue,
    Take care!
And what she says, it is not true,
    Beware! Beware!
    Trust her not,
She is fooling thee!

She has a bosom as white as snow,
    Take care!
She knows how much it is best to show,
    Beware! Beware!
    Trust her not,
She is fooling thee!

She gives thee a garland woven fair,
    Take care !
It is a fool's-cap for thee to wear,
    Beware ! Beware !
    Trust her not,
She is fooling thee !

OLIVER WENDELL HOLMES
1809 – 1894

CONTENTMENT

"*Man wants but little here below*"

LITTLE I ask; my wants are few;
   I only wish a hut of stone,
(A *very plain* brown stone will do,)
   That I may call my own;
And close at hand is such a one,
In yonder street that fronts the sun.

Plain food is quite enough for me;
   Three courses are as good as ten; —
If nature can subsist on three,
   Thank Heaven for three. Amen!
I always thought cold victuals nice; —
My *choice* would be vanilla ice.

I care not much for gold or land; —
   Give me a mortgage here and there, —
Some good bank-stock, — some note of hand,
   Or trifling railroad share, —
I only ask that Fortune send
A *little* more than I shall spend.

Honors are silly toys, I know,
   And titles are but empty names;
I would *perhaps* be Plenipo, —
   But only near St. James;
I'm very sure I should not care
To fill our Gubernator's chair.

Jewels are baubles; 't is a sin
   To care for such unfruitful things; —
One good-sized diamond in a pin, —
   Some, *not so large*, in rings, —
A ruby, and a pearl or so,
Will do for me; — I laugh at show.

My dame should dress in cheap attire
   (Good heavy silks are never dear;) —
I own perhaps I *might* desire
   Some shawls of true cashmere, —
Some marrowy crapes of China silk,
Like wrinkled skins on scalded milk.

I would not have the horse I drive
   So fast that folks must stop and stare;
An easy gate, — two forty-five, —
   Suits me; I do not care; —
Perhaps, for just a *single spurt*,
Some seconds less would do no hurt.

Of pictures, I should like to own
   Titians and Raphaels three or four, —
I love so much their style and tone, —
   One Turner, and no more,
(A landscape, — foreground golden dirt, —
The sunshine painted with a squirt).

Of books but few, — some fifty score
   For daily use and bound for wear;
The rest upon an upper floor; —
    Some *little* luxury *there*
Of red morocco's gilded gleam,
And vellum rich as country cream.

Busts, cameos, gems, — such things as these,
   Which others often show for pride,
I value for their power to please,
    And selfish churls deride; —
One Stradivarius, I confess,
Two Meerschaums I would fain possess.

Wealth's wasteful tricks I will not learn,
   Nor ape the glittering upstart fool; —
Shall not carved tables serve my turn,
    But *all* must be of buhl?
Give grasping pomp its double share, —
I ask but *one* recumbent chair.

Thus humble let me live and die,
   Not long for Midas' golden touch;
If Heaven more generous gifts deny,
    I shall not miss them *much*, —
Too grateful for the blessing lent
Of simple tastes and mind content!

TO AN INSECT

I LOVE to hear thine earnest voice,
 Wherever thou art hid,
Thou testy little dogmatist,
 Thou pretty Katydid!
Thou mindest me of gentle folks, —
 Old gentlefolks are they, —
Thou say'st an undisputed thing
 In such a solemn way.

Thou art a female, Katydid!
 I know it by the trill
That quivers through thy piercing notes,
 So petulant and shrill.
I think there is a knot of you
 Beneath the hollow tree, —
A knot of spinster Katydids, —
 Do Katydids drink tea?

O tell me where did Katy live,
 And what did Katy do?
And was she very fair and young,
 And yet so wicked, too?
Did Katy love a naughty man,
 Or kiss more cheeks than one?
I warrant Katy did no more
 Than many a Kate has done.

Dear me! I'll tell you all about
 My fuss with little Jane,
And Ann, with whom I used to walk
 So often down the lane,

And all that tore their locks of black,
    Or wet their eyes of blue, —
Pray tell me, sweetest Katydid,
    What did poor Katy do?

Ah no! the living oak shall crash,
    That stood for ages still,
The rock shall rend its mossy base
    And thunder down the hill,
Before the little Katydid
    Shall add one word, to tell
The mystic story of the maid
    Whose name she knows so well.

Peace to the ever-murmuring race!
    And when the latest one
Shall fold in death her feeble wings
    Beneath the autumn sun,
Then shall she raise her fainting voice,
    And lift her drooping lid,
And then the child of future years
    Shall hear what Katy did.

THE LAST LEAF

I SAW him once before,
As he passed by the door,
    And again
The pavement stones resound,
As he totters o'er the ground
    With his cane.

They say that in his prime,
Ere the pruning-knife of Time
    Cut him down,
Not a better man was found
By the Crier on his round
    Through the town.

But now he walks the streets,
And he looks at all he meets
    Sad and wan,
And he shakes his feeble head,
That it seems as if he said,
    "They are gone."

The mossy marbles rest
On the lips that he has prest
    In their bloom,
And the names he loved to hear
Have been carved for many a year
    On the tomb.

My grandmamma has said —
Poor old lady, she is dead
    Long ago —
That he had a Roman nose,
And his cheek was like a rose
    In the snow;

But now his nose is thin,
And it rests upon his chin
    Like a staff,
And a crook is in his back,
And a melancholy crack
    In his laugh.

I know it is a sin
For me to sit and grin
    At him here;
But the old three-cornered hat,
And the breeches, and all that,
    Are so queer!

And if I should live to be
The last leaf upon the tree
    In the spring,
Let them smile, as I do now,
At the old forsaken bough
    Where I cling.

ON LENDING A PUNCH-BOWL

THIS ancient silver bowl of mine, it tells of good old times,
Of joyous days and jolly nights, and merry Christmas chimes;
They were a free and jovial race, but honest, brave, and true,
Who dipped their ladle in the punch when this old bowl was new.

A Spanish galleon brought the bar, — so runs the ancient tale;
'T was hammered by an Antwerp smith, whose arm was like a flail;
And now and then between the strokes, for fear his strength should fail,
He wiped his brow and quaffed a cup of good old Flemish ale.

'T was purchased by an English squire to please his loving dame,
Who saw the cherubs, and conceived a longing for the same;
And oft as on the ancient stock another twig was found,
'T was filled with caudle spiced and hot, and handed smoking round.

But, changing hands, it reached at length a Puritan divine,
Who used to follow Timothy, and take a little wine,
But hated punch and prelacy; and so it was, perhaps,
He went to Leyden, where he found conventicles and schnapps.

And then, of course, you know what's next: it left the
 Dutchman's shore
With those that in the Mayflower came, — a hundred souls
 and more, —
Along with all the furniture, to fill their new abodes, —
To judge by what is still on hand, at least a hundred loads.

'T was on a dreary winter's eve, the night was closing dim,
When brave Miles Standish took the bowl, and filled it to
 the brim ;
The little Captain stood and stirred the posset with his
 sword,
And all his sturdy men-at-arms were ranged about the
 board.

BILL AND JOE

COME, dear old comrade, you and I
  Will steal an hour from days gone by,
The shining days when life was new,
And all was bright with morning dew,
The lusty days of long ago,
When you were Bill and I was Joe.

Your name may flaunt a titled trail
Proud as a cockerel's rainbow tail,
And mine as brief appendix wear
As Tam O'Shanter's luckless mare;
To-day, old friend, remember still
That I am Joe and you are Bill.

You 've won the great world's envied prize,
And grand you look in people's eyes,
With H O N. and LL. D.
In big brave letters, fair to see, —
Your fist, old fellow! off they go! —
How are you, Bill? How are you, Joe?

You 've worn the judge's ermined robe;
You 've taught your name to half the globe;
You 've sung mankind a deathless strain;
You 've made the dead past live again:
The world may call you what it will,
But you and I are Joe and Bill.

The chaffing young folks stare and say
  "See those old buffers, bent and gray, —
They talk like fellows in their teens!
Mad, poor old boys! That 's what it means," —

And shake their heads; they little know
The throbbing hearts of Bill and Joe! —

How Bill forgets his hour of pride,
While Joe sits smiling at his side;
How Joe, in spite of time's disguise,
Finds the old schoolmate in his eyes, —
Those calm, stern eyes that melt and fill
As Joe looks fondly up at Bill.

Ah, pensive scholar, what is fame?
A fitful tongue of leaping flame;
A giddy whirlwind's fickle gust,
That lifts a pinch of mortal dust;
A few swift years, and who can show
Which dust was Bill and which was Joe?

The weary idol takes his stand,
Holds out his bruised and aching hand,
While gaping thousands come and go, —
How vain it seems, this empty show!
Till all at once his pulses thrill; —
'Tis poor old Joe's " God bless you, Bill!"

And shall we breathe in happier spheres
The names that pleased our mortal ears,
In some sweet lull of harp and song
For earth-born spirits none too long,
Just whispering of the world below
Where this was Bill and that was Joe?

No matter; while our home is here
No sounding name is half so dear;
When fades at length our lingering day,
Who cares what pompous tombstones say?
Read on the hearts that love us still,
Hic jacet Joe.   *Hic jacet* Bill.

DOROTHY Q

A FAMILY PORTRAIT

GRANDMOTHER'S mother: her age, I guess,
Thirteen summers, or something less;
Girlish bust, but womanly air;
Smooth, square forehead with uprolled hair;
Lips that lover has never kissed;
Taper fingers and slender wrist;
Hanging sleeves of stiff brocade;
So they painted the little maid.

On her hand a parrot green
Sits unmoving and broods serene.
Hold up the canvas full in view, —
Look! there 's a rent the light shines through,
Dark with a century's fringe of dust, —
That was a Red-Coat's rapier-thrust!
Such is the tale the lady old,
Dorothy's daughter's daughter, told.

Who the painter was none may tell, —
One whose best was not over well;
Hard and dry, it must be confessed,
Flat as a rose that has long been pressed;
Yet in her cheek the hues are bright,
Dainty colors of red and white,
And in her slender shape are seen
Hint and promise of stately mien.

Look not on her with eyes of scorn, —
Dorothy Q. was a lady born!
Ay! since the galloping Normans came,
England's annals have known her name;

And still to the three-hilled rebel town
Dear is that ancient name's renown,
For many a civic wreath they won,
The youthful sire and the gray-haired son.

O Damsel Dorothy! Dorothy Q.!
Strange is the gift that I owe to you;
Such a gift as never a king
Save to daughter or son might bring, —
All my tenure of heart and hand,
All my title to house and land;
Mother and sister and child and wife
And joy and sorrow and death and life!

What if a hundred years ago
Those close-shut lips had answered No,
When forth the tremulous question came
That cost the maiden her Norman name,
And under the folds that look so still
The bodice swelled with the bosom's thrill?
Should I be I, or would it be
One tenth another, to nine tenths me?

Soft is the breath of a maiden's Yes:
Not the light gossamer stirs with less;
But never a cable that holds so fast
Through all the battles of wave and blast,
And never an echo of speech or song
That lives in the babbling air so long!
There were tones in the voice that whispered then
You may hear to-day in a hundred men.

O lady and lover, how faint and far
Your images hover, — and here we are,
Solid and stirring in flesh and bone, —
Edward's and Dorothy's — all their own, —

A goodly record for Time to show
Of a syllable spoken so long ago ! —
Shall I bless you, Dorothy, or forgive
For the tender whisper that bade me live?

It shall be a blessing, my little maid !
I will heal the stab of the Red-Coat's blade,
And freshen the gold of the tarnished frame,
And gild with a rhyme your household name ;
So you shall smile on us brave and bright
As first you greeted the morning's light,
And live untroubled by woes and fears
Through a second youth of a hundred years.

FRANCES SARGENT OSGOOD
1811 – 1850

A DANCING GIRL

SHE comes — the spirit of the dance !
   And but for those large, eloquent eyes,
Where passion speaks in every glance,
   She 'd seem a wanderer from the skies.

So light that, gazing breathless there,
   Lest the celestial dream should go,
You 'd think the music in the air
   Waved the fair vision to and fro !

Or that the melody's sweet flow
   Within the radiant creature play'd,
And those soft wreathing arms of snow
   And white sylph feet the music made.

Now gliding slow with dreamy grace,
   Her eyes beneath their lashes lost,
Now motionless, with lifted face,
   And small hands on her bosom cross'd.

And now with flashing eyes she springs —
   Her whole bright figure raised in air,
As if her soul had spread its wings
   And poised her one wild instant there !

She spoke not; but, so richly fraught
   With language are her glance and smile,
That, when the curtain fell, I thought
   She had been talking all the while.

JOHN GODFREY SAXE
1816 – 1887

THE MOURNER À LA MODE

I SAW her last night at a party
   (The elegant party at Mead's),
And looking remarkably hearty
   For a widow so young in her weeds;
Yet I know she was suffering sorrow
   Too deep for the tongue to express, —
Or why had she chosen to borrow
   So much from the language of dress?

Her shawl was as sable as night;
   And her gloves were as dark as her shawl;
And her jewels — that flashed in the light —
   Were black as a funeral pall;
Her robe had the hue of the rest,
   (How nicely it fitted her shape!)
And the grief that was heaving her breast
   Boiled over in billows of crape!

What tears of vicarious woe,
   That else might have sullied her face,
Were kindly permitted to flow
   In ripples of ebony lace!
While even her fan, in its play,
   Had quite a lugubrious scope,
And seemed to be waving away
   The ghost of the angel of Hope!

Yet rich as the robes of a queen
    Was the sombre apparel she wore;
I 'm certain I never had seen
    Such a sumptuous sorrow before;
And I could n't help thinking the beauty,
    In mourning the loved and the lost,
Was doing her conjugal duty
    Altogether regardless of cost!

One surely would say a devotion
    Performed at so vast an expense
Betrayed an excess of emotion
    That was really something immense;
And yet as I viewed, at my leisure,
    Those tokens of tender regard,
I thought: — It is scarce without measure —
    The sorrow that goes by the yard!

Ah! grief is a curious passion;
    And yours — I am sorely afraid
The very next phase of the fashion
    Will find it beginning to fade;
Though dark are the shadows of grief,
    The morning will follow the night,
Half-tints will betoken relief,
    Till joy shall be symboled in white!

Ah well! it were idle to quarrel
    With Fashion, or aught she may do;
And so I conclude with a moral
    And metaphor — warranted new: —
When *measles* come handsomely out,
    The patient is safest, they say;
And the *Sorrow* is mildest, no doubt,
    That works in a similar way!

THE HEART AND THE LIVER

MUSINGS OF A DYSPEPTIC

I

SHE'S broken-hearted, I have heard, —
  Whate'er may be the reason;
(Such things will happen now and then
  In Love's tempestuous season;)
But still I marvel she should show
  No plainer outward token,
If such a vital inward part
  Were very badly broken!

II

She's broken-hearted, I am told,
  And so, of course, believe it;
When truth is fairly certified
  I modestly receive it;
But after such an accident,
  It surely is a blessing,
It does n't in the least impair
  Her brilliant style of dressing!

III

She's broken-hearted: who can doubt
  The noisy voice of Rumor?
And yet she seems — for such a wreck —
  In no unhappy humor;
She sleeps (I hear) at proper hours,
  When other folks are dozy;
Her eyes are sparkling as of yore,
  And still her cheeks are rosy!

IV

She's broken-hearted, and they say
　　She never can recover;
And then — in not the mildest way —
　　They blame some fickle lover;
I know she's dying — by degrees —
　　But, sure as I'm a sinner,
I saw her eat, the other day,
　　A most prodigious dinner!

V

Alas! that I, in idle rhyme,
　　Should e'er profanely question
(As I have done while musing o'er
　　My chronic indigestion)
If one should not receive the blow
　　With blessings on the Giver,
That only falls upon the heart,
　　And kindly spares the LIVER!

LITTLE JERRY, THE MILLER

A BALLAD

BENEATH the hill you may see the mill
  Of wasting wood and crumbling stone;
The wheel is dripping and clattering still,
  But Jerry, the miller, is dead and gone.

Year after year, early and late,
  Alike in summer and winter weather,
He pecked the stones and calked the gate,
  And mill and miller grew old together.

"Little Jerry!" — 't was all the same, —
  They loved him well who called him so;
And whether he 'd ever another name,
  Nobody ever seemed to know.

'T was, "Little Jerry, come grind my rye;"
  And "Little Jerry, come grind my wheat;"
And "Little Jerry" was still the cry,
  From matron bold and maiden sweet.

'T was "Little Jerry" on every tongue,
  And so the simple truth was told;
For Jerry was little when he was young,
  And Jerry was little when he was old.

But what in size he chanced to lack,
  That Jerry made up in being strong;
I 've seen a sack upon his back
  As thick as the miller, and quite as long.

Always busy, and always merry,
　　Always doing his very best,
A notable wag was Little Jerry,
　　Who uttered well his standing jest.

How Jerry lived is known to fame,
　　But how he died there's none may know;
One autumn day the rumor came,
　　"The brook and Jerry are very low."

And then 't was whispered, mournfully,
　　The leech had come, and he was dead;
And all the neighbors flocked to see;
　　"Poor Little Jerry!" was all they said.

They laid him in his earthy bed, —
　　His miller's coat his only shroud;
"Dust to dust," the parson said,
　　And all the people wept aloud.

For he had shunned the deadly sin,
　　And not a grain of over-toll
Had ever dropped into his bin,
　　To weigh upon his parting soul.

Beneath the hill there stands the mill,
　　Of wasting wood and crumbling stone;
The wheel is dripping and clattering still,
　　But Jerry, the miller, is dead and gone.

MY FAMILIAR

" Ecce iterum Crispinus! "

I

AGAIN I hear that creaking step! —
  He's rapping at the door! —
Too well I know the boding sound
    That ushers in a bore.
I do not tremble when I meet
    The stoutest of my foes,
But Heaven defend me from the friend
    Who comes — but never goes!

II

He drops into my easy-chair,
    And asks about the news;
He peers into my manuscript,
    And gives his candid views;
He tells me where he likes the line,
    And where he's forced to grieve
He takes the strangest liberties, —
    But never takes his leave!

III

He reads my daily paper through
    Before I've seen a word;
He scans the lyric (that I wrote)
    And thinks it quite absurd;

He calmly smokes my last cigar,
    And coolly asks for more;
He opens everything he sees —
    Except the entry door!

IV

He talks about his fragile health,
    And tells me of the pains
He suffers from a score of ills
    Of which he ne'er complains;
And how he struggled once with death
    To keep the fiend at bay;
On themes like those away he goes, —
    But never goes away!

V

He tells me of the carping words
    Some shallow critic wrote;
And every precious paragraph
    Familiarly can quote;
He thinks the writer did me wrong;
    He'd like to run him through!
He says a thousand pleasant things, —
    But never says, "Adieu!"

VI

Whene'er he comes, — that dreadful man, —
    Disguise it as I may,
I know that, like an Autumn rain,
    He'll last throughout the day.
In vain I speak of urgent tasks;
    In vain I scowl and pout;
A frown is no extinguisher, —
    It does not put him out!

VII

I mean to take the knocker off,
    Put crape upon the door,
Or hint to John that I am gone
    To stay a month or more.
I do not tremble when I meet
    The stoutest of my foes,
But Heaven defend me from the friend
    Who never, never goes!

EARLY RISING

"GOD bless the man who first invented sleep!"
   So Sancho Panza said, and so say I:
And bless him also that he did n't keep
   His great discovery to himself; nor try
To make it — as the lucky fellow might —
A close monopoly by patent-right.

Yes — bless the man who first invented sleep,
   (I really can't avoid the iteration;)
But blast the man, with curses loud and deep,
   Whate'er the rascal's name, or age, or station,
Who first invented, and went round advising,
That artificial cut-off — Early Rising!

"Rise with the lark, and with the lark to bed,"
   Observes some solemn, sentimental owl;
Maxims like these are very cheaply said;
   But, ere you make yourself a fool or fowl,
Pray just inquire about his rise and fall,
And whether larks have any beds at all!

The time for honest folks to be a-bed
   Is in the morning, if I reason right;
And he who cannot keep his precious head
   Upon his pillow till it's fairly light,
And so enjoy his forty morning winks,
Is up to knavery; or else — he drinks!

Thompson, who sung about the "Seasons," said
  It was a glorious thing to *rise* in season;
But then he said it — lying — in his bed,
  At ten o'clock A.M., — the very reason
He wrote so charmingly. The simple fact is
His preaching was n't sanctioned by his practice.

'T is, doubtless, well to be sometimes awake, —
  Awake to duty, and awake to truth, —
But when, alas! a nice review we take
  Of our best deeds and days, we find, in sooth,
The hours that leave the slightest cause to weep
Are those we passed in childhood or asleep!

'T is beautiful to leave the world awhile
  For the soft visions of the gentle night;
And free, at last, from mortal care or guile,
  To live as only in the angels' sight,
In sleep's sweet realm so cosily shut in,
Where, at the worst, we only *dream* of sin!

So let us sleep, and give the Maker praise.
  I like the lad who, when his father thought
To clip his morning nap by hackneyed phrase
  Of vagrant worm by early songster caught,
Cried, "Served him right! — it 's not at all surprising;
The worm was punished, sir, for early rising!"

THOMAS WILLIAM PARSONS
1819–1892

HEALTH AND WEALTH AND LOVE AND LEISURE, AND A HAPPY NEW YEAR, TO MY SWEET LADYE

IN the fair blank that now, like some new bay
In life's vague ocean, opens with to-day,
Couldst thou but write, dear lady, at thy will,
All thou wouldst choose of good, or shun of ill,
As on this paper thou mayst fill the space
With thoughts and wishes gentle as thy face,
Thou couldst not crowd the days that are to be
With happier fortune than I hope for thee.

For, if the saint that keeps the book above
Which holds the record of thy life and love,
Where at one view thy childhood and thine age,
Thy past and future, gleam upon the page,
Shouldst trust his volume to my hand, and say,
Write for Augusta all you ask or pray,
All that twelve moons may bring of peace and bliss,
Then would I register some fate like this:

Health, first of all, that every morn may find
The same bright casket for the same clear mind,
And every night bring such repose, that care
May find no triumph in one altered hair.

Affection then, the same thou still hast known,
Such as would shudder at a careless tone,
And count it selfishness to have a grief
That in thy sharing did not seek relief.

Next golden leisure, to enjoy the sun,
With one to worship, and but only one;
With him to tread the solitude, and then
No less securely try the ways of men;
To move in crowds, yet keep the calm within,
Still amid noise, and spotless amid sin.

ST. VALENTINE'S DAY

THIS day was sacred, once, to Pan,
    And kept with song and wine;
But when our better creed began
    'T was held no more divine,
Until there came a holy man,
    One Bishop Valentine.

He, finding, as all good men will,
    Much in the ancient way
That was not altogether ill,
    Restored the genial day,
And we the pagan fashion still
    With pious hearts obey.

Without this custom, all would go
    Amiss in Love's affairs;
All passion would be poor dumb show,
    Pent sighs, and secret prayers;
And bashful maids would never know
    What timid swain was theirs.

Ah! many things with mickle pains
    Without reward are done;
A thousand poets rack their brains
    For her who loves but one;
Yea, many weary with their strains
    The nymph that cares for none.

Yet, should no faithful heart be faint
    To give affection's sign;
So, dearest, let mine own acquaint
    With its emotions — thine;
And blessings on that fine old saint,
    Good Bishop Valentine!

IN RETURN FOR SOME PRAIRIE BIRDS

'T IS a pretty fair farm, that of ours in the West;
  And the poultry they raise there, it equals the best;
These hens of the prairie, I never have seen
A civilized capon more plump or as clean.

'T is a fine hunting-ground, the domain we possess,
Some thousand miles off, — sure it cannot be less;
For it took 'em three days, in the mire and the snow,
These birds to bring hither, — the rivers were low.

I have walked over England, and given a look
At all their great houses; but ne'er was a duke,
For all his French pedigree, all his fair crest,
That had such a park as our park in the West.

Gray bird of the wilderness! lucky for you
That you 'scaped the fell shaft of the wandering Sioux!
Then the savage had gorged you, half burnt and half raw,
And tossed your sweet bones a *bonne bouche* to his squaw.

But now you shall grace an Athenian board,
And sparkling libations to you shall be poured;
If Iowa send game and Ohio send wine,
And Cambridge good company, — may we not dine?

What have they at Windsor we cannot have here?
If we 've no royal names, yet we 'll have royal cheer:
This only is wanting, — that he were my guest
Whose friendship supplies me with birds from the West.

JAMES RUSSELL LOWELL
1819 – 1891

AUF WIEDERSEHEN

SUMMER

THE little gate was reached at last,
   Half hid in lilacs down the lane;
She pushed it wide, and, as she past,
A wistful look she backward cast,
   And said, — "*Auf wiedersehen!*"

With hand on latch, a vision white
   Lingered reluctant, and again
Half doubting if she did aright,
Soft as the dews that fell that night,
   She said, — "*Auf wiedersehen!*"

The lamp's clear gleam flits up the stair;
   I linger in delicious pain;
Ah, in that chamber, whose rich air
To breathe in thought I scarcely dare,
   Thinks she, — "*Auf wiedersehen!*"

'T is thirteen years; once more I press
   The turf that silences the lane;
I hear the rustle of her dress,
I smell the lilacs, and — ah, yes,
   I hear, — "*Auf wiedersehen!*"

Sweet piece of bashful maiden art!
　The English words had seemed too fain,
But these — they drew us heart to heart,
Yet held us tenderly apart;
　She said, — "*Auf wiedersehen!*"

WITHOUT AND WITHIN

MY coachman, in the moonlight there,
    Looks through the side-light of the door;
I hear him with his brethren swear,
    As I could do, — but only more.

Flattening his nose against the pane,
    He envies me my brilliant lot,
Breathes on his aching fists in vain,
    And dooms me to a place more hot.

He sees me into supper go,
    A silken wonder by my side,
Bare arms, bare shoulders, and a row
    Of flounces, for the door too wide.

He thinks how happy is my arm
    'Neath its white-gloved and jewelled load;
And wishes me some dreadful harm,
    Hearing the merry corks explode.

Meanwhile I inly curse the bore
    Of hunting still the same old coon,
And envy him, outside the door,
    In golden quiets of the moon.

The winter wind is not so cold
    As the bright smile he sees me win,
Nor the host's oldest wine so old
    As our poor gabble sour and thin.

I envy him the ungyved prance
   By which his freezing feet he warms,
And drag my lady's-chains and dance
   The galley-slave of dreary forms.

O, could he have my share of din,
   And I his quiet! — past a doubt
'T would still be one man bored within,
   And just another bored without.

ALADDIN

WHEN I was a beggarly boy,
   And lived in a cellar damp,
I had not a friend nor a toy,
   But I had Aladdin's lamp;
When I could not sleep for cold,
   I had fire enough in my brain,
And builded, with roofs of gold,
   My beautiful castles in Spain!

Since then I have toiled day and night,
   I have money and power good store,
But I 'd give all my lamps of silver bright,
   For the one that is mine no more;
Take, Fortune, whatever you choose,
   You gave, and may snatch again;
I have nothing 't would pain me to lose,
   For I own no more castles in Spain!

AN EMBER PICTURE

How strange are the freaks of memory!
    The lessons of life we forget,
While a trifle, a trick of color,
    In the wonderful web is set, —

Set by some mordant of fancy,
    And, spite of the wear and tear
Of time or distance or trouble,
    Insists on its right to be there.

A chance had brought us together;
    Our talk was of matters-of-course;
We were nothing, one to the other,
    But a short half-hour's resource.

We spoke of French acting and actors,
    And their easy, natural way:
Of the weather, for it was raining
    As we drove home from the play.

We debated the social nothings
    We bore ourselves so to discuss;
The thunderous rumors of battle
    Were silent the while for us.

Arrived at her door, we left her
    With a drippingly hurried adieu,
And our wheels went crunching the gravel
    Of the oak-darkened avenue.

As we drove away through the shadow,
  The candle she held in the door
From rain-varnished tree-trunk to tree-trunk
  Flashed fainter, and flashed no more ; —

Flashed fainter, then wholly faded
  Before we had passed the wood ;
But the light of the face behind it
  Went with me and stayed for good.

The vision of scarce a moment,
  And hardly marked at the time,
It comes unbidden to haunt me,
  Like a scrap of ballad-rhyme.

Had she beauty? Well, not what they call so ;
  You may find a thousand as fair ;
And yet there's her face in my memory
  With no special claim to be there.

As I sit sometimes in the twilight,
  And call back to life in the coals
Old faces and hopes and fancies
  Long buried, (good rest to their souls !)

Her face shines out in the embers ;
  I see her holding the light,
And hear the crunch of the gravel
  And the sweep of the rain that night.

'T is a face that can never grow older,
  That never can part with its gleam,
'T is a gracious possession forever,
  For is it not all a dream?

THE NIGHTINGALE IN THE STUDY

"COME forth!" my catbird calls to me,
    "And hear me sing a cavatina
That, in this old familiar tree,
    Shall hang a garden of Alcina.

"These buttercups shall brim with wine
    Beyond all Lesbian juice or Massic;
May not New England be divine?
    My ode to ripening summer classic?

"Or, if to me you will not hark,
    By Beaver Brook a thrush is ringing
Till all the alder-coverts dark
    Seem sunshine-dappled with his singing.

"Come out beneath the unmastered sky,
    With its emancipating spaces,
And learn to sing as well as I,
    Without premeditated graces.

"What boot your many-volumned gains,
    Those withered leaves forever turning,
To win, at best, for all your pains,
    A nature mummy-wrapt in learning?

"The leaves wherein true wisdom lies
    On living trees the sun are drinking;
Those white clouds, drowsing through the skies,
    Grew not so beautiful by thinking.

"Come out! with me the oriole cries,
　　Escape the demon that pursues you!
And, hark, the cuckoo weatherwise,
　　Still hiding, farther onward wooes you."

"Alas, dear friend, that, all my days,
　　Has poured from that syringa thicket
The quaintly discontinuous lays
　　To which I hold a season-ticket,

"A season-ticket cheaply bought
　　With a dessert of pilfered berries,
And who so oft my soul hast caught
　　With morn and evening voluntaries,

"Deem me not faithless, if all day
　　Among my dusty books I linger,
No pipe, like thee, for June to play
　　With fancy-led, half-conscious finger.

"A bird is singing in my brain
　　And bubbling o'er with mingled fancies,
Gay, tragic, rapt, right heart of Spain
　　Fed with the sap of old romances.

"I ask no ampler skies than those
　　His magic music rears above me,
No falser friends, no truer foes, —
　　And does not Doña Clara love me?

"Cloaked shapes, a twanging of guitars,
　　A rush of feet, and rapiers clashing,
Then silence deep with breathless stars,
　　And overhead a white hand flashing.

"O music of all moods and climes,
　　Vengeful, forgiving, sensuous, saintly,
Where still, between the Christian chimes,
　　The moorish cymbal tinkles faintly!

" O life borne lightly in the hand,
   For friend or foe with grace Castilian !
O valley safe in Fancy's land,
   Not trampled to mud yet by the million !

" Bird of to-day, thy songs are stale
   To his, my singer of all weathers,
My Calderon, my nightingale,
   My Arab soul in Spanish feathers.

" Ah, friend, these singers dead so long,
   And still, God knows, in purgatory,
Give its best sweetness to all song,
   To Nature's self her better glory."

THE PETITION

OH, tell me less or tell me more,
  Soft eyes with mystery at the core,
That always seem to meet my own
Frankly as pansies fully blown,
Yet waver still 'tween no and yes!

So swift to cavil and deny,
Then parley with concessions shy,
Dear eyes, that share their youth with mine
And through my inmost shadows shine,
Oh, tell me more or tell me less!

IN ARCADIA

[*Read at the Meeting of the Papyrus Club*]

I, WALKING the familiar street,
    While a crammed horse-car tinkled through it,
Was lifted from my prosy feet
    And in Arcadia ere I knew it.

Fresh sward for gravel soothed my tread,
    And shepherds' pipes my ear delighted;
The riddle may be lightly read:
    I met two lovers newly plighted.

They murmured by in happy care,
    New plans for paradise devising.
Just as the moon with pensive stare
    O'er Mistress Craigie's pines was rising.

Astarte, known nigh three-score years,
    Me to no speechless rapture urges;
Them, in Elysium she enspheres,
    Queen, from of old, of thaumaturges.

The railings put forth bud and bloom,
    The house fronts all with myrtles twine them,
And light-winged Loves in every room
    Make nests, and then with kisses line them.

O sweetness of untasted life!
    O dream, its own supreme fulfilment!
O hours with all illusion rife,
    As ere the heart divined what ill meant!

"Et ego," sighed I to myself,
   And strove some vain regrets to bridle.
"Though now laid dusty on the shelf,
   Was hero once of such an idyl!

"An idyl ever newly sweet,
   Although since Adam's day recited,
Whose measures time them to Love's feet,
   Whose sense is every ill requited."

Maiden, if I may counsel, drain
   Each drop of this enchanted season,
For even our honeymoons must wane,
   Convicted of green cheese by Reason.

And none will seem so safe from change,
   Nor in such skies benignant hover,
As this, beneath whose witchery strange
   You tread on rose leaves with your lover.

The glass unfilled all tastes can fit,
   As round its brim Conjecture dances,
For not Mephisto's self hath wit
   To draw such vintages as Fancy's.

When our pulse beats its minor key,
   When play-time halves and school-time doubles,
Age fills the cup with serious tea
   Which one Dame Clicquot starred with bubbles.

"Fie, Mr. Lowell, is this wise?
   Is this the mortal of a poet,
Who, when the plant of Eden dies,
   Is privileged once more to sow it?

"That herb of clay-disdaining root,
   From stars secreting what it feeds on,
Is burnt-out passion's slag and soot
   Fit soil to sow its dainty seeds on?

"Pray why, if in Arcadia once,
  Need one so soon forget the way there?
Or why, once there, be such a dunce
  As not contentedly to stay there?"

Dear child, 't is but a sorry jest,
  And from my heart I hate the cynic
Who makes the Book of Life a nest
  For comments staler than rabbinic.

If Love his simple spell but keep,
  Life with ideal eyes to flatter,
The Grail itself was crockery cheap
  To Everyday's communion platter.

One Darby is to me well known
  Who, as the hearth between blazes,
Sees the old moonlight shine on Joan
  And float her youthward in its hazes,

He rubs his spectacles, he stares —
  'T is the same face that witched him early!
He feels for his remaining hairs —
  Is this a fleece that feels so curly?

"Good heavens! but now 't is winter gray,
  And I of years had more than plenty;
The almanac 's a fool! 'T is May!
  Hang family Bibles! I am twenty!

"Come, Joan, your arm; we'll walk the room —
  The lane, I mean — do you remember?
How confident the roses bloom,
  As if it ne'er could be December!

"No more it shall, while in your eyes
  My heart its summer heat recovers,
And you, howe'er your mirror lies,
  Find your old beauty in your lover's."

THOMAS DUNN ENGLISH
1819 – 1902

KATE VANE

I WELL remember when at morn
    We twain to school would go,
In summer heat, in winter chill —
    Unheeding sun or snow.
I think of when I used to gaze
Within your bonnet on those days —
Perchance to steal a kiss, Kate Vane.
Ah, would that we were young again!

I think of when I "did the sums"
    That puzzled so your pate,
And, when I went to say my task,
    Slipped in your hands the slate.
Oft would I claim and get for this
What now were worth a world — a kiss:
You did not think it harm, Kate Vane —
Ah, would that we were young again!

I think of when the brindle cow
    Adown the cattle track
Chased you, and I with stick and stone
    In triumph beat her back.
Your little cheek was on my breast,
Your little lips to mine were prest,
Your eyes were filled with love, Kate Vane —
Ah, would that we were young again!

I think of when I halved with you
    My cherished, childish store,
And only wished, for your dear sake,
    It might be ten times more.
Our schoolmates, in their petty strife
With us, would call us "man and wife;"
None call us that just now, Kate Vane —
Ah, would that we were young again!

I see you now when years have passed,
    And find you full as fair;
Time has not soiled your purity,
    Nor marked your face with care.
I love you as I did before —
Yea! deeper, stronger, better, more.
What! are you in my arms, Kate Vane?
Dear love, we both are young again!

WILLIAM WETMORE STORY
1819 – 1895

DO YOU REMEMBER

"Un Bacio Dato Non e Mai Perduto"

BECAUSE we once drove together
  In the moonlight over the snow,
With the sharp bells ringing their tinkling chime,
  So many a year ago,

So, now, as I hear them jingle,
  The winter comes back again,
Though the summer stirs in the heavy trees,
  And the wild rose scents the lane.

We gather our furs around us,
  Our faces the keen air stings,
And noiseless we fly o'er the snow-hushed world
  Almost as if we had wings.

Enough is the joy of mere living,
  Enough is the blood's quick thrill;
We are simply happy — I care not why —
  We are happy beyond our will.

The trees are with icicles jewelled,
    The walls are o'er-surfed with snow;
The houses with marble whiteness are roofed,
    In their windows the home-lights glow.

Through the tense, clear sky above us
    The keen stars flash and gleam,
And wrapped in their silent shroud of snow
    The broad fields lie and dream.

And jingling with low, sweet clashing
    Ring the bells as our good horse goes,
And tossing his head, from his nostrils red
    His frosty breath he blows.

And close you nestle against me,
    While around your waist my arm
I have slipped — 't is so bitter, bitter cold —
    It is only to keep us warm.

We talk, and then we are silent;
    And suddenly — you know why —
I stooped — could I help it? You lifted your face —
    We kissed — there was nobody nigh.

And no one was ever the wiser,
    And no one was ever the worse;
The skies did not fall — as perhaps they ought —
    And we heard no paternal curse.

I never told it — did you, dear? —
    From that day unto this;
But my memory keeps in its inmost recess,
    Like a perfume, that innocent kiss.

I dare say you have forgotten,
    'T was so many a year ago;
Or you may not choose to remember it,
    Time may have changed you so.

The world so chills us and kills us,
   Perhaps you may scorn to recall
That night, with its innocent impulse —
   Perhaps you 'll deny it all.

But if of that fresh, sweet nature
   The veriest vestige survive,
You remember that moment's madness —
   You remember that moonlight drive.

A MUSICAL BOX

I KNOW her, the thing of laces, and silk,
  And ribbons, and gauzes, and crinoline,
With her neck and shoulders as white as milk,
  And her doll-like face and conscious mien.
A lay-figure fashioned to fit a dress,
  All stuffed within with straw and bran;
Is that a woman to love, to caress?
  Is that a creature to charm a man?

Only listen! how charmingly she talks
  Of your dress and hers — of the Paris mode —
Of the coming ball — of the opera-box —
  Of jupons, and flounces, and fashions abroad.
Not a bonnet in church but she knows it well,
  And Fashion she worships with downcast eyes;
A marchande de modes is her oracle,
  And Paris her earthly paradise.

She's perfect to whirl with in a waltz;
  And her shoulders show well on a soft divan,
As she lounges at night and spreads her silks,
  And plays with her bracelets and flirts her fan;
With a little laugh at whatever you say,
  And rounding her "No" with a look of surprise:
And lisping her "Yes," with an air distrait,
  And a pair of aimless, wandering eyes.

Her duty this Christian never omits!
  She makes her calls, and she leaves her cards,
And enchants a circle of half-fledged wits,
  And slim attachés and six-foot Guards.

Her talk is of people, who 're nasty or nice,
  And she likes little bon-bons of compliments;
While she seasons their sweetness by way of spice,
  By some witless scandal she often invents.

Is this the thing for a mother or wife?
  Could love ever grow on such barren rocks?
Is this a companion to take for a wife?
  One might as well marry a musical box.
You exhaust in a day her full extent;
  'T is the same little tinkle of tunes always;
You must wind her up with a compliment,
  To be bored with the only airs she plays.

SNOWDROP

WHEN, full of warm and eager love,
    I clasp you in my fond embrace,
You gently push me back and say,
    "Take care, my dear, you 'll spoil my lace."

You kiss me just as you would kiss
    Some woman friend you chanced to see;
You call me "dearest." — All love's forms
    Are yours, not its reality.

Oh Annie! cry, and storm, and rave!
    Do anything with passion in it!
Hate me an hour, and then turn round
    And love me truly, just one minute.

JAMES THOMAS FIELDS
1820 – 1881

THE SEARCH

"GIVE me the girl whose lips disclose,
Whene'er she speaks, rare pearls in rows,
And yet whose words more genuine are
Than pearls or any shining star.

"Give me those silvery tones that seem
An angel's singing in a dream, —
A presence beautiful to view,
A seraph's, yet a woman's too.

"Give me that one whose temperate mind
Is always toward the good inclined,
Whose deeds spring from her soul unsought, —
Twin-born of grace and artless thought; —

"Give me that spirit, — seek for her
To be my constant minister!"
Dear friend, — I heed your earnest prayers, —
I'll call your lovely wife down-stairs.

MABEL, IN NEW HAMSPHIRE

FAIREST of the fairest, rival of the rose,
That is *Mabel of the Hills*, as everybody knows.

Do you ask me near what stream this sweet floweret grows?
That's an ignorant question, sir, as everybody knows.

Ask you what her age is, reckoned as time goes?
Just the age of beauty, as everybody knows.

Is she tall as Rosalind, standing on her toes?
She is just the perfect height, as everybody knows.

What's the color of her eyes, when they ope or close?
Just the color they should be, as everybody knows.

Is she lovelier dancing, or resting in repose?
Both are radiant pictures, as everybody knows.

Do her ships go sailing on every wind that blows?
She is richer far than that, as everybody knows.

Has she scores of lovers, heaps of bleeding beaux?
That question's quite superfluous, as everybody knows.

I could tell you something, if I only chose! —
But what's the use of telling what everybody knows?

PETER REMSEN STRONG
1822 – 1878

"AWFUL!"

I WAS dining at Delmonico's, a week or two ago,
With a charming little maiden and her dapper little beau;
And I tried, by close attention, as I trifled with my fork,
To arrive at a solution of the meaning of their talk.

It was all about a party, which, they said, was "awful jolly,"
Where their "awful pretty" hostess had an "awful handsome Dolly;"
And an "awful cunning necklace," which her "awful good papa"
Had procured for her at Tiffany's, while shopping with mamma.

Yet 't would seem there was a drawback to the pleasures of the fête,
For the "awful stylish" Reginald arrived "so awful late,"
And the "awful swell" arrangement of his "awful nice" cravat,
And his "awful lovely" waistcoat did n't compensate for that.

Then he flirted — "oh, 't was awful!" — with that "awful little minx"
Who was dancing, after supper, to the strains of "Captain Jinks;"
And he paid such "awful compliments" — 't was really quite absurd —
Just the "awfullest of nonsense that a creature ever heard."

I listened, quite bewildered by the babble of the pair,
Who were sitting at the table, with a very quiet air;
And I thought, "My little darlings, if your soup were half as hot
Or as potent as your language, it would kill you on the spot!

"Now, if such a thing should happen, though you'd make an 'awful' end,
'T would be fitting retribution for your usage of a friend —
A grave and solemn Adjective — true Saxon to the core —
Who should meet with proper treatment, not be forced to prove a bore.

"I confess, it sorely puzzles me, to think what you would say,
If a something *really awful* were to happen in your way;
For I'm sure, with simple English, you would never be content,
But your thoughts, in foreign expletives, would have to find a vent."

While musing in this fashion, (feeling rather cross and old,)
I forgot about my dinner, which was getting "awful" cold;
And the adjective kept dropping from the lips of either child,
Till with "awful," "Awful," "AWFUL" I was fairly driven wild.

CHARLES GODFREY LELAND
1824–1903

EVA

I'VE seen bright eyes like mountain lakes,
    Reflecting heaven's blue;
And some like black volcano-gulfs,
    With wildfire flashing through;

But thine are like the eternal skies,
    Which draw the soul afar —
Their every glance a meteor,
    And every thought a star.

Some lips when robbed seem cherries sweet,
    — Small sin to those who stole
But thine are like the Eden fruit,
    Whose theft may cost a soul.

Oh, coral fruit of Paradise!
    Who would not grasp the prize?
With heaven so near to bring him back,
    In those eternal eyes.

THELEMÉ

I SAT one night on a palace step
   Wrapped up in a mantle thin,
And I gazed with a smile on the world without,
   With a growl at my world within.
Till I heard the merry voices ring
   Of a lordly companie,
And straight to myself I began to sing:
   "It is there I ought to be."

And long I gazed through a lattice raised,
   Which looked from the old grey wall,
And my glance went in with the evening breeze,
   And ran o'er the revellers all.
And I said: "If they saw me 't would cool their mirth
   Far more than this wild breeze free;
But a merrier party was ne'er on earth,
   And among them I ought to be."

And, oh, but they all were beautiful,
   Fairer than fairy dreams,
And their words were sweet as the wind-harp's tone
   When it sings o'er summer streams;
And they pledged each other with noble mien,
   "True heart, with my life to thee!"
"Alack!" quoth I, "but my soul is dry,
   And among them I fain would be."

And the gentlemen were noble souls,
    Good fellows both sain and sound:
I had not deemed that a band like this
    Could over the world be found;
And they spoke of brave and beautiful things,
    Of all that was dear to me;
So I thought, "Perhaps they would like me well
    If among them I once might be!"

And lovely were the ladies too
    Who sat in the lighted hall,
And one there was, oh, dream of life!
    The loveliest of them all;
She sat alone by an empty chair,
    The Queen of the feast was she;
And I said to myself, "By that lady fair
    I certainly ought to be!"

And aloud she spoke: "We have waited long
    For one who in fear and doubt
Looks wistfully into our Hall of Song,
    As he sits on the steps without;
I have sung to him long in silent dreams,
    I have led him o'er land and sea:
Go, welcome him in as his rank beseems,
    And give him a place by me!"

They opened the door, yet I shrunk with shame
    As I sat in my mantle thin,
But they haled me out with a joyous shout,
    And merrily led me in,
And gave me a place by my bright-haired love
    As she wept with joy and glee,
So I said to myself: "By the stars above,
    I am just where I ought to be!"

Farewell to thee, life of joy and grief!
  Farewell to thee, care and pain!
Farewell, thou cruel and selfish world,
  For I never will know thee again!
I live in a land where good fellows abound, —
  In Thelemé by the sea;
They may long for a happier life that will, —
  I am just where I ought to be.

RICHARD HENRY STODDARD
1825 – 1903

[*From " The Poems of R. H. Stoddard."* Copyright, *1880, by Charles Scribner's Sons*]

THE FLOWER OF LOVE LIES BLEEDING

I MET a little maid one day,
   All in the bright May weather;
She danced, and brushed the dew away
   As lightly as a feather.
She had a ballad in her hand
   That she had just been reading,
But was too young to understand : —
That ditty of a distant land,
   " The flower of love lies bleeding."

She tripped across the meadow grass,
   To where a brook was flowing,
Across the brook like wind did pass, —
   Wherever flowers were growing
Like some bewildered child she flew,
   Whom fairies were misleading :
" Whose butterfly," I said, " are you?
And what sweet thing do you pursue ? " —
   " The flower of love lies bleeding ! "

"I've found the wild rose in the hedge,
  I've found the tiger-lily, —
The blue flag by the water's edge, —
  The dancing daffodilly, —
King-cups and pansies, — every flower
  Except the one I'm needing; —
Perhaps it grows in some dark bower,
And opens at a later hour, —
  This flower of love lies bleeding."

"I wouldn't look for it," I said,
  "For you can do without it:
There's no such flower." She shook her head;
  "But I have read about it!"
I talked to her of bee and bird,
  But she was all unheeding:
Her tender heart was strangely stirred,
She harped on that unhappy word, —
  "The flower of love lies bleeding!"

"My child," I sighed, and dropped a tear,
  "I would no longer mind it;
You'll find it some day, never fear,
  For all of us must find it!
I found it many a year ago,
  With one of gentle breeding;
You and the little lad you know, —
I see why you are weeping so, —
  Your flower of love lies bleeding!"

THE DIVAN

A LITTLE maid of Astrakan,
    An idol on a silk divan;
She sits so still, and never speaks,
    She holds a cup of mine;
'T is full of wine, and on her cheeks
    Are stains and smears of wine.

Thou little girl of Astrakan,
I join thee on the silk divan:
There is no need to seek the land,
    The rich bazars where rubies shine;
For mines are in that little hand,
    And on those little cheeks of thine.

JOHN TOWNSEND TROWBRIDGE
1827 –

PLEASANT STREET

'TIS Pleasant, indeed,
    As the letters read
On the guideboard at the crossing.
    Over the street
    The branches meet,
Gently swaying and tossing.

    Through its leafy crown
    The sun strikes down
In wavering flakes and flashes,
    As winding it goes
    Betwixt tall rows
Of maples and elms and ashes.

    There, high aloof
    In the gilded roof,
Are the pewee and vireo winging
    Their fitful flight
    In the flickering light;
The hangbird's basket swinging.

    By many a great
    And small estate,
And orchard cool and pleasant,
    And croquet-ground,
    The way sweeps round,
In many a curve and crescent.

  In crescents and curves
  It sways and swerves,
Like the flow of a stately river.
  On carriage and span,
  On maiden and man,
The dappling sunbeams quiver.

  It winds between
  Broad slopes of the green
Wood-mantled and shaggy highland,
  And shores that rise
  From the lake, which lies
Below, with its one fair island.

  The long days dawn
  Over lake and lawn,
And set on the hills; and at even
  Above it beam
  All the lights that gleam
In the starry streets of heaven.

  But not for these,
  Lake, lawns and trees,
And gardens gay in their season, —
  Its praise I sing
  For a sweeter thing,
And a far more human reason.

  Children I meet
  In house and street,
Pretty maids and happy mothers,
  All fair to see;
  But one to me
More beautiful than all others!

  One whose pure face,
  With its glancing grace,
Makes every one her lover;

Charming the sight
With a sweeter light
Than falls from the boughs above her.

Though on each side
Are the homes of pride,
And of beauty, — here and there one, —
The dearest of all,
Though simple and small,
Is the dwelling of my fair one.

You will marvel that such
A gay sprite so much
Of a grave man's life engages,
And smile when I
Confess with a sigh
The difference in our ages.

Must love depart
With our youth, and the heart,
As we grow in years, become colder?
My love is but four,
While I am twoscore,
And may be a trifle older.

With her smile and her glance,
And her curls that dance,
No one could ever resist her.
If anywhere
There's another so fair,
Why, that must be her sister.

With screams of glee
At the sight of me,
Together forth they sally
From under the boughs
That screen the house
That stands beside the valley.

It is scenes like these,
As they clasp my knees
And clamor for kiss and present,
That still must make
Our street by the lake
More pleasant — oh, most pleasant!

Ride merrily past,
Glide smoothly and fast,
O throngs of wealth and of pleasure!
While sober and slow
On foot I go,
Enjoying my humble leisure.

O world, before
My lowly door
Daily coming and going;
O tide of life,
O stream of strife,
Forever ebbing and flowing!

By the show and the shine
No eye can divine
If you be fair or hateful;
I only know,
As you come and go,
That I am glad and grateful.

So here, well back
From the shaded track,
By the curve of its greenest crescent,
To-day I swing
In my hammock, and sing
The praise of the street named PLEASANT.

FITZ JAMES O'BRIEN
1828 – 1862

ON THE PASSAIC

WHERE the river seeks the cover
    Of the trees whose boughs hang over,
And the slopes are green with clover,
   In the quiet month of May;
Where the eddies meet and mingle,
Babbling o'er the stony shingle,
      There I angle,
      There I dangle,
      All the day.

Oh, 't is sweet to feel the plastic
Rod, with top and butt elastic,
Shoot the line in coils fantastic,
   Till, like thistle-down, the fly
Lightly drops upon the water,
Thirsting for the finny slaughter,
      As I angle,
      And I dangle,
      Mute and sly.

Then I gently shake the tackle,
Till the barbed and fatal hackle
In its tempered jaws shall shackle
   That old trout, so wary grown.

Now I strike him! joy ecstatic!
Scouring runs! leaps acrobatic!
    So I angle,
    So I dangle,
      All alone.

Then when grows the sun too fervent,
And the lurking trouts, observant,
Say to me, "Your humble servant!
  Now we see your treacherous hook!"
Maud, as if by hazard wholly,
Saunters down the pathway slowly,
    While I angle,
    There to dangle
      With her hook.

Then somehow the rod reposes,
And the hook no page uncloses;
But I read the leaves of roses
  That unfold upon her cheek;
And her small hand, white and tender,
Rests in mine! Ah! what can send her
    Thus to dangle,
    While I angle?
      Cupid, speak!

CHARLES GRAHAM HALPINE
1829–1868

FEMININE ARITHMETIC

LAURA

ON me he shall ne'er put a ring,
   So, mamma, 't is in vain to take trouble —
For I was but eighteen in spring,
   While his age exactly is double.

MAMMA

He 's but in his thirty-sixth year,
   Tall, handsome, good-natured and witty,
And should you refuse him, my dear,
   May you die an old maid without pity!

LAURA

His figure, I grant you, will pass,
   And at present he 's young enough plenty;
But when I am sixty, alas!
   Will not he be a hundred and twenty?

QUAKERDOM

THE FORMAL CALL

THROUGH her forced, abnormal quiet,
    Flashed the soul of frolic riot,
And a most malicious laughter lighted up her downcast
    eyes;
    All in vain I tried each topic,
    Ranged from polar climes to tropic —
Every commonplace I started met with yes-or-no replies

    For her mother — stiff and stately,
    As if starched and ironed lately —
Sat erect, with rigid elbows bedded thus in curving palms;
    There she sat on guard before us,
    And in words precise, decorous,
And most calm, reviewed the weather, and recited several
    psalms.

    How without abruptly ending
    This my visit, and offending
Wealthy neighbors, was the problem which employed my
    mental care;
    When the butler, bowing lowly,
    Uttered clearly, stiffly, slowly,
"Madam, please, the gardener wants you" — Heaven, I
    thought, has heard my prayer.

    "Pardon me!" she grandly uttered;
    Bowing low, I gladly muttered,
"Surely, madam!" and, relieved, I turned to scan the
    daughter's face.

Ha! what pent-up mirth outflashes
From beneath those penciled lashes!
How the drill of Quaker custom yields to Nature's brilliant
    grace.

Brightly springs the prisoned fountain
From the side of Delphi's mountain
When the stone that weighed upon its buoyant life is thrust
    aside ;
So the long-enforced stagnation
Of the maiden's conversation
Now imparted five-fold brilliance to its ever-varying tide.

Widely ranging, quickly changing,
Witty, winning, from beginning
Unto end I listened, merely flinging in a casual word ;
Eloquent, and yet how simple!
Hand and eye, and eddying dimple,
Tongue and lip together made a music seen as well as
    heard.

When the noonday woods are ringing,
All the birds of summer singing,
Suddenly there falls a silence, and we know a serpent nigh :
So upon the door a rattle
Stopped our animated tattle,
And the stately mother found us prim enough to suit her eye.

HENRY TIMROD

1829 – 1867

A TRIFLE

I KNOW not why, but ev'n to me
My songs seem sweet when read to thee.

Perhaps in this the pleasure lies —
I read my thoughts within thine eyes.

And so dare fancy that my art
May sink as deeply as thy heart.

Perhaps I love to make my words
Sing round thee like so many birds,

Or, maybe, they are only sweet
As they seem offerings at thy feet.

Or haply, Lily, when I speak,
I think, perchance, they touch thy cheek,

Or with a yet more precious bliss,
Die on thy red lips in a kiss.

Each reason here — I cannot tell —
Or all perhaps may solve the spell.

But if she watch when I am by,
Lily may deeper see than I.

SILAS WEIR MITCHELL
1829 –

A DECANTER OF MADEIRA, AGED 86, TO GEORGE BANCROFT, AGED 86, GREETING

GOOD Master, you and I were born
In " Teacup days " of hoop and hood,
And when the silver cue hung down,
And toasts were drunk, and wine was good ;

When kin of mine (a jolly brood)
From sideboards looked, and knew full well
What courage they had given the beau,
How generous made the blushing belle.

Ah me ! what gossip could I prate
Of days when doors were locked at dinners !
Believe me, I have kissed the lips
Of many pretty saints — or sinners.

Lip service have I done, alack !
I don't repent, but come what may,
What ready lips, sir, I have kissed,
Be sure at least I shall not say.

Two honest gentlemen are we, —
I Demi John, whole George are you ;
When Nature grew us one in years
She meant to make a generous brew.

She bade me store for festal hours
The sun our south-side vineyard knew;
To sterner tasks she set your life,
As statesman, writer, scholar, grew.

Years eighty-six have come and gone;
At last we meet. Your health to-night.
Take from this board of friendly hearts
The memory of a proud delight.

The days that went have made you wise,
There's wisdom in my rare bouquet.
I'm rather paler than I was;
And, on my soul, you're growing gray.

I like to think, when Toper Time
Has drained the last of me and you,
Some here shall say, They both were good, —
The wine we drank, the man we knew.

EDMUND CLARENCE STEDMAN
1833 –

PAN IN WALL STREET

JUST where the Treasury's marble front
   Looks over Wall Street's mingled nations;
Where Jews and Gentiles most are wont
   To throng for trade and last quotations;
Where, hour by hour, the rates of gold
   Outrival, in the ears of people,
The quarter-chimes, serenely tolled
   From Trinity's undaunted steeple, —

Even there I heard a strange, wild strain
   Sound high above the modern clamor,
Above the cries of greed and gain,
   The curbstone war, the auction's hammer;
And swift, on Music's misty ways,
   It led, from all this strife for millions,
To ancient, sweet-do-nothing days
   Among the kirtle-robed Sicilians.

And as it stilled the multitude,
   And yet more joyous rose, and shriller,
I saw the minstrel, where he stood
   At ease against a Doric pillar:
One hand a droning organ played,
   The other held a Pan's-pipe (fashioned
Like those of old) to lips that made
   The reeds give out that strain impassioned.

'T was Pan himself had wandered here
    A-strolling through this sordid city,
And piping to the civic ear
    The prelude of some pastoral ditty!
The demigod had crossed the seas, —
    From haunts of shepherd, nymph, and satyr,
And Syracusan times, — to these
    Far shores and twenty centuries later.

A ragged cap was on his head;
    But — hidden thus — there was no doubting
That, all with crispy locks o'erspread,
    His gnarlèd horns were somewhere sprouting;
His club-feet, cased in rusty shoes,
    Were crossed, as on some frieze you see them,
And trousers, patched of divers hues,
    Concealed his crooked shanks beneath them.

He filled the quivering reeds with sound,
    And o'er his mouth their changes shifted,
And with his goat's-eyes looked around
    Where'er the passing current drifted;
And soon, as on Trinacrian hills
    The nymphs and herdsmen ran to hear him,
Even now the tradesmen from their tills,
    With clerks and porters, crowded near him.

The bulls and bears together drew
    From Jauncey Court and New Street Alley,
As erst, if pastorals be true,
    Came beasts from every wooded valley;
The random passers stayed to list, —
    A boxer Ægon, rough and merry,
A Broadway Daphnis, on his tryst
    With Nais at the Brooklyn Ferry.

A one-eyed Cyclops halted long
    In tattered cloak of army pattern,
And Galatea joined the throng, —
    A blowsy, apple-vending slattern;
While old Silenus staggered out
    From some new-fangled lunch-house handy,
And bade the piper, with a shout,
    To strike up Yankee Doodle Dandy!

A newsboy and a peanut-girl
    Like little Fauns began to caper:
His hair was all in tangled curl,
    Her tawny legs were bare and taper;
And still the gathering larger grew,
    And gave its pence and crowded nigher,
While aye the shepherd-minstrel blew
    His pipe, and struck the gamut higher.

O heart of Nature, beating still
    With throbs her vernal passion taught her,
Even here, as on the vine-clad hill,
    Or by the Arethusan water!
New forms may fold the speech, new lands
    Arise within these ocean-portals,
But Music waves eternal wands, —
    Enchantress of the souls of mortals!

So thought I, — but among us trod
    A man in blue, with legal baton,
And scoffed the vagrant demigod,
    And pushed him from the step I sat on.
Doubting I mused upon the cry,
    "Great Pan is dead!" — and all the people
Went on their ways: — and clear and high
    The quarter sounded from the steeple.

PROVENÇAL LOVERS

AUCASSIN AND NICOLETTE

WITHIN the garden of Beaucaire
   He met her by a secret stair, —
The night was centuries ago.
Said Aucassin, "My love, my pet,
These old confessors vex me so!
They threaten all the pains of hell
Unless I give you up, ma belle;" —
Said Aucassin to Nicolette.

"Now, who should there in Heaven be
To fill your place, ma très-douce mie?
To reach that spot I little care!
There all the droning priests are met;
All the old cripples, too, are there
That unto shrines and altars cling
To filch the Peter-pence we bring;" —
Said Aucassin to Nicolette.

"There are the barefoot monks and friars
With gowns well tattered by the briars,
The saints who lift their eyes and whine:
I like them not — a starveling set!
Who'd care with folk like these to dine?
The other road 't were just as well
That you and I should take, ma belle!" —
Said Aucassin to Nicolette.

"To purgatory I would go
With pleasant comrades whom we know,
Fair scholars, minstrels, lusty knights
Whose deeds the land will not forget,

The captains of a hundred fights,
The men of valor and degree :
We'll join that gallant company," —
Said Aucassin to Nicolette.

"There, too, are jousts and joyance rare,
And beauteous ladies debonair,
The pretty dames, the merry brides,
Who with their wedded lords coquette
And have a friend or two besides, —
And all in gold and trappings gay,
With furs, and crests in vair and gray ; "
Said Aucassin to Nicolette.

"Sweet players on the cithern strings,
And they who roam the world like kings,
Are gathered there, so blithe and free !
Pardie ! I'd join them now, my pet,
If you went also, ma douce mie !
The joys of heaven I'd forego
To have you with me there below," —
Said Aucassin to Nicolette.

COUSIN LUCRECE

HERE where the curfew
    Still, they say, rings,
Time rested long ago,
    Folding his wings;
Here, on old Norwich's
    Out-along road
Cousin Lucretia
    Had her abode.

Norridge, not Nor-wich
    (See Mother Goose),
Good enough English
    For a song's use.
Side and roof shingled,
    All of a piece,
Here was the cottage
    Of Cousin Lucrece.

Living forlornly
    On nothing a year,
How she took comfort
    Does not appear;
How kept her body,
    On what they gave,
Out of the poor-house,
    Out of the grave.

Highly connected?
    Straight as the Nile
Down from "the Gard'ners"
    Of Gardiner's Isle;

(Three bugles, chevron gules,
    Hand upon sword),
Great-great-granddaughter
    Of the third lord.

Bent almost double,
    Deaf as a witch,
Gout her chief trouble —
    Just as if rich;
Vain of her ancestry,
    Mouth all agrin,
Nose half-way meeting her
    Sky-pointed chin.

Ducking her forehead-top,
    Wrinkled and bare,
With a colonial
    Furbelowed air
Greeting her next of kin,
    Nephew and niece, —
Foolish old, prating old
    Cousin Lucrece.

Once every year she had
    All she could eat:
Turkey and cranberries,
    Pudding and sweet;
Every Thanksgiving,
    Up to the great
House of her kinsman, was
    Driven in state.

Oh, what a sight to see,
    Rigged in her best!
Wearing the famous gown
    Drawn from her chest, —

Worn, ere King George's reign
 Here chanced to cease,
Once by a forbear
 Of Cousin Lucrece.

Damask brocaded,
 Cut very low;
Short sleeves and finger-mitts
 Fit for a show;
Palsied neck shaking her
 Rust-yellow curls,
Rattling its roundabout
 String of mock pearls;

Over her noddle,
 Draggled and stark,
Two ostrich feathers —
 Brought from the ark.
Shoes of frayed satin,
 All heel and toe,
On her poor crippled feet
 Hobbled below.

My! how the Justice's
 Sons and their wives
Laughed; while the little folk
 Ran for their lives,
Asking if beldames
 Out of the past,
Old fairy godmothers,
 Always could last?

No! One Thanksgiving,
 Bitterly cold,
After they took her home
 (Ever so old),
In her great chair she sank,
 There to find peace;
Died in her ancient dress —
 Poor old Lucrece.

FUIT ILIUM

ONE by one they died, —
  Last of all their race;
Nothing left but pride,
  Lace and buckled hose.
Their quietus made,
  On their dwelling-place
Ruthless hands are laid:
  Down the old house goes!

See the ancient manse
  Meet its fate at last!
Time, in his advance,
  Age nor honor knows;
Axe and broadaxe fall,
  Lopping off the Past:
Hit with bar and maul,
  Down the old house goes!

Sevenscore years it stood:
  Yes, they built it well,
Though they built of wood,
  When that house arose.
For its cross-beams square
  Oak and walnut fell;
Little worse for wear,
  Down the old house goes!

Rending board and plank,
  Men with crowbars ply,
Opening fissures dank,
  Striking deadly blows.

From the gabled roof
   How the shingles fly!
Keep you here aloft, —
   Down the old house goes!

Holding still its place,
   There the chimney stands,
Stanch from top to base,
   Frowning on its foes.
Heave apart the stones,
   Burst its iron bands!
How it shakes and groans!
   Down the old house goes!

Round the mantelpiece
   Glisten Scripture tiles;
Henceforth they shall cease
   Painting Egypt's woes,
Painting David's fight,
   Fair Bathsheba's smiles,
Blinded Samson's night, —
   Down the old house goes!

On these oaken floors
   High-shoed ladies trod;
Through those panelled doors
   Trailed their furbelows;
Long their day has ceased;
   Now, beneath the sod,
With the worms they feast,
   Down the old house goes!

Many a bride has stood
   In yon spacious room;
Here her hand was wooed
   Underneath the rose;

O'er that sill the dead
  Reached the family tomb:
All, that were, have fled, —
  Down the old house goes!

Once, in yonder hall,
  Washington, they say,
Led the New-Year's ball,
  Stateliest of beaux.
Oh that minuet,
  Maids and matrons gay!
Are there such sights yet?
  Down the old house goes!

British troopers came
  Ere another year,
With their coats aflame,
  Mincing on their toes;
Daughters of the house
  Gave them haughty cheer,
Laughed to scorn their vows, —
  Down the old house goes!

Doorway high the box
  In the grass-plot spreads;
It has borne its locks
  Through a thousand snows;
In an evil day,
  From those garden-beds
Now 't is hacked away, —
  Down the old house goes!

Lo! the sycamores,
  Scathed and scrawny mates,
At the mansion doors
  Shiver, full of woes;

With its life they grew,
  Guarded well its gates;
Now their task is through, —
  Down the old house goes!

On this honored site
  Modern trade will build, —
What unseemly fright
  Heaven only knows!
Something peaked and high,
  Smacking of the guild:
Let us heave a sigh, —
  Down the old house goes!

RICHARD REALF
1834-1878

SUNBEAM AND I

WE own no houses, no lots, no lands,
   No dainty viands for us are spread;
By sweat of our brows and toil of our hands
   We earn the pittance that buys us bread.
And yet we live in a nobler state —
   Sunbeam and I — than the millionaires
Who dine off silvern and golden plate,
   With liveried lacqueys behind their chairs.

We have no riches in bonds or stocks,
   No bank books show our balance to draw;
Yet we carry a safe key that unlocks
   More treasures than Crœsus ever saw.
We wear no velvets or satins fine,
   We dress in a very homely way;
But O, what luminous lusters shine
   About Sunbeam's gowns and my hodden gray.

No harp, no dulcimer, no guitar
   Breaks into singing at Sunbeam's touch;
But do not think that our evenings are
   Without their music; there is none such
In the concert halls where the lyric air
   In palpitant billows swims and swoons;
Our lives are as psalms, and our foreheads wear
   The calms of the hearts of perfect Junes.

When we walk together (we do not ride,
   We are far too poor), it is very rare
We are bowed unto from the other side
   Of the street — but not for this do we care.
We are not lonely; we pass along,
   Sunbeam and I — and you cannot see
(We can) what tall and beautiful throng
   Of Angels we have for company.

When cloudy weather obscures our skies,
   And some days darken with drops of rain,
We have but to look at each other's eyes,
   And all is balmy and bright again.
Ah! ours is the alchemy that transmutes
   The dregs to elixir, the dross to gold;
And so we live on Hesperean fruits,
   Sunbeam and I — and never grow old.

Never grow old, and we dwell in peace,
   And love our fellows and envy none;
And our hearts are glad at the large increase
   Of plenteous virtue under the sun.
And the days go by with their thoughtful tread,
   And the shadows lengthen toward the West,
But the wane of our young years brings no dread
   To harm our harvests of quiet rest.

Sunbeam's hair will be streaked with gray,
   And Time will furrow my darling's brow;
But never can Time's hand take away
   The tender halo that clasps it now.
So we dwell in wonderful opulence,
   With nothing to hurt us, nor upbraid;
And my life trembles with reverence,
   And Sunbeam's spirit is not afraid.

GEORGE ARNOLD
1834 – 1865

BEER

HERE
  With my beer
I sit,
While golden moments flit:
Alas!
They pass
Unheeded by:
And, as they fly,
I,
Being dry,
Sit, idly sipping here
My beer.

O, finer far
Than fame, or riches, are
The graceful smoke-wreaths of this free cigar!
  Why
  Should I
  Weep, wail, or sigh?
  What if luck has passed me by?
What if my hopes are dead, —
My pleasures fled?
  Have I not still
  My fill
Of right good cheer, —
Cigars and beer?

  Go, whining youth,
  Forsooth!
Go, weep and wail,
Sigh and grow pale,
  Weave melancholy rhymes
  On the old times,
Whose joys like shadowy ghosts appear,
But leave to me my beer!
  Gold is dross, —
  Love is loss, —
So, if I gulp my sorrows down,
Or see them drown
In foamy draughts of old nut-brown,
Then do I wear the crown,
  Without the cross!

THE JOLLY OLD PEDAGOGUE

'TWAS a jolly old pedagogue, long ago,
    Tall and slender, and sallow and dry;
His form was bent, and his gait was slow,
His long, thin hair was as white as snow,
    But a wonderful twinkle shone in his eye;
And he sang every night as he went to bed,
    "Let us be happy down here below;
The living should live, though the dead be dead,"
    Said the jolly old pedagogue, long ago.

He taught his scholars the rule of three,
    Writing, and reading, and history, too;
He took the little ones up on his knee,
For a kind old heart in his breast had he,
    And the wants of the littlest child he knew:
"Learn while you 're young," he often said,
    "There is much to enjoy, down here below;
Life for the living, and rest for the dead!"
    Said the jolly old pedagogue, long ago.

With the stupidest boys he was kind and cool,
    Speaking only in gentlest tones;
The rod was hardly known in his school, —
Whipping, to him, was a barbarous rule,
    And too hard work for his poor old bones;
Beside, it was painful, he sometimes said:
    "We should make life pleasant, down here below,
The living need charity more than the dead,"
    Said the jolly old pedagogue, long ago.

He lived in the house by the hawthorn lane,
  With roses and woodbine over the door;
His rooms were quiet, and neat, and plain,
But a spirit of comfort there held reign,
  And made him forget he was old and poor;
" I need so little," he often said;
  " And my friends and relatives here below
Won't litigate over me when I am dead,"
  Said the jolly old pedagogue, long ago.

But the pleasantest times that he had, of all,
  Were the sociable hours he used to pass,
With his chair tipped back to a neighbor's wall,
Making an unceremonious call,
  Over a pipe and a friendly glass:
This was the finest pleasure, he said,
  Of the many he tasted, here below;
" Who has no cronies, had better be dead!"
  Said the jolly old pedagogue, long ago.

Then the jolly old pedagogue's wrinkled face
  Melted all over in sunshiny smiles;
He stirred his glass with an old-school grace,
Chuckled, and sipped, and prattled apace,
  Till the house grew merry, from cellar to tiles:
" I'm a pretty old man," he gently said,
  " I have lingered a long while, here below;
But my heart is fresh, if my youth is fled!"
  Said the jolly old pedagogue, long ago.

He smoked his pipe in the balmy air,
  Every night when the sun went down,
While the soft wind played in his silvery hair,
Leaving its tenderest kisses there,
  On the jolly old pedagogue's jolly old crown:

And, feeling the kisses, he smiled, and said,
    'T was a glorious world, down here below;
" Why wait for happiness till we are dead?"
    Said the jolly old pedagogue, long ago.

He sat at his door, one midsummer night,
    After the sun had sunk in the west,
And the lingering beams of golden light
Made his kindly old face look warm and bright,
    While the odorous night-wind whispered, " Rest!"
Gently, gently, he bowed his head. . .
    There were angels waiting for him, I know;
He was sure of happiness, living or dead,
    This jolly old pedagogue, long ago!

YOUTH AND AGE

YOUTH hath many charms, —
  Hath many joys, and much delight;
Even its doubts, and vague alarms,
  By contrast make it bright:
And yet — and yet — forsooth,
  I love Age as well as Youth!

Well, since I love them both,
  The good of both I will combine, —
In women, I will look for Youth,
  And look for Age, in wine:
And then — and then — I'll bless
This twain that gives me happiness!

CHARLES HENRY WEBB

1834 –

THE KING AND THE POPE

THE King and the Pope together
  Have written a letter to me;
It is signed with a golden sceptre,
It is sealed with a golden key.
The King wants me out of his eyesight;
The Pope wants me out of his See.

The King and the Pope together
Have a hundred acres of land:
I do not own the foot of ground
On which my two feet stand;
But the prettiest girl in the kingdom
Strolls with me on the sand.

The King has a hundred yeomen
Who will fight for him any day,
The Pope has priests and bishops
Who for his soul will pray:
I have only one little sweetheart,
But she 'll kiss me when I say.

The King is served at his table
By ladies of high degree;
The Pope has never a true love,
So a cardinal pours his tea:
No ladies stand round me in waiting,
But my sweetheart sits by me.

And the King with his golden sceptre,
The Pope with Saint Peter's key,
Can never unlock the one little heart
That is opened only to me.
For I am the Lord of a Realm,
And I am the Pope of a See ;
Indeed, I 'm supreme in the kingdom
That is sitting just now on my knee !

DICTUM SAPIENTI

THAT 't is well to be off with the old love
    Before one is on with the new
Has somehow passed into a proverb, —
    But I never have found it true.

No love can be quite like the old love,
    Whate'er may be said for the new —
And if you dismiss me, my darling,
    You may come to this thinking, too.

Were the proverb not wiser if mended,
    And the fickle and wavering told
To be sure they 're on with the new love
    Before they are off with the old?

WITH A ROSEBUD

THIS fair rosebud, Elsie, see,
    Gathered by my hand for thee —
While the morning yet was new,
And its leaves still wet with dew.
It may die — but if for thee,
Who would not the rosebud be?
Shall I tell thee to my thought
Whom its fresh young beauty brought —
Conscious that in turn to thee
It can bring no thought of me?
By this token know, young maid,
Rosebuds are not all that fade.
Wouldst thou quite believe, if told,
That I was not always old?
Yet the floweret prithee take;
Wear it for the giver's sake.
Though it breathe to thee in sooth,
But of beauty, now, and youth,
When it fades into the sear,
It may then suggest me, dear.

WITH A ROSE

LADY, lest they should betray,
On thy lips this rose I lay.

Not its petals to surprise
With a hue that theirs outvies,

Not to shame them to confess
Fragrance of the Rose is less —

Only with a rose to seal
Rosebud lips, lest they reveal —

Faint unfolding, in their sleep —
What a rose's heart should keep.

Eden since, no wizard knows
Spell that bindeth like the rose —

Flower of Love, the last to leave,
Bud that blossomed first for Eve.

With my rose for lock and key
None shall pick thy lips, pardie!

But to me if they unclose —
All is safe beneath the rose.

WHAT SHE SAID ABOUT IT

LYRICS to Inez and Jane,
    Dolores and Ethel and May;
Señoritas distant as Spain,
    And damsels just over the way!

It is not that I'm jealous, not that,
    Of either Dolores or Jane,
Of some girl in an opposite flat,
    Or in one of his castles in Spain,

But it is that salable prose
    Put aside for this profitless strain,
I sit the day darning his hose —
    And he sings of Dolores and Jane.

Though the winged-horse must caracole free —
    With the pretty, when "spurning the plain,"
Should the team-work fall wholly on me
    While he soars with Dolores and Jane?

I am neither Dolores nor Jane,
    But to lighten a little my life
Might the Poet not spare me a strain —
    Although I am only his wife!

DUM VIVIMUS VIGILAMUS

TURN out more ale, turn up the light;
I will not go to bed to-night.
Of all the foes that man should dread
The first and worst one is a bed.
Friends I have had both old and young,
And ale we drank and songs we sung:
Enough you know when this is said,
That, one and all, — they died in bed.
   In bed they died and I'll not go
   Where all my friends have perished so.
   Go you who glad would buried be,
   But not to-night a bed for me.

For me to-night no bed prepare,
But set me out my oaken chair.
And bid no other guests beside
The ghosts that shall around me glide;
In curling smoke-wreaths I shall see
A fair and gentle company.
Though silent all, rare revellers they,
Who leave you not till break of day.
   Go you who would not daylight see,
   But not to-night a bed for me:
   For I've been born and I've been wed —
   All of man's peril comes of bed.

And I'll not seek — whate'er befall —
Him who unbidden comes to all.
A grewsome guest, a lean-jawed wight —
God send he do not come to-night!
But if he do, to claim his own,
He shall not find me lying prone;

But blithely, bravely, sitting up,
And raising high the stirrup-cup.
  Then if you find a pipe unfilled,
  An empty chair, the brown ale spilled ;
  Well may you know, though naught be said,
  That I 've been borne away to bed.

WILLIAM HENRY VENABLE
1836 –

THE SCHOOL GIRL

FROM some sweet home, the morning train
    Brings to the city,
Five days a week, in sun or rain,
Returning like a song's refrain,
    A school girl pretty.

A wild flower's unaffected grace
    Is dainty miss's;
Yet in her shy, expressive face
The touch of urban arts I trace, —
    And artifices.

No one but she and Heaven knows
    Of what she 's thinking:
It may be either books or beaux,
Fine scholarship or stylish clothes,
    Per cents or prinking.

How happy must the household be,
    This morn that kissed her;
Not every one can make so free;
Who sees her, inly wishes she
    Were his own sister.

How favored is the book she cons,
    The slate she uses,
The hat she lightly doffs and dons,
The orient sunshade that she owns,
    The desk she chooses!

Is she familiar with the wars
    Of Julius Cæsar?
Do crucibles and Leyden jars,
And French, and earth, and sun, and stars,
    And Euclid, please her?

She studies music, I opine;
    O day of knowledge!
And all the other arts divine,
Of imitation and design,
    Taught in the college.

A charm attends her everywhere, —
    A sense of beauty;
Care smiles to see her free of cares;
The hard heart loves her unawares;
    Age pays her duty.

She is protected by the sky;
    Good spirits tend her;
Her innocence is panoply;
God's wrath must on the miscreant lie
    Who dares offend her!

THE TUNES DAN HARRISON USED TO PLAY

OFTTIMES when recollections throng
    Serenely back from childhood's years,
Awaking thoughts that slumbered long,
    Compelling smiles or starting tears,
The music of a violin
Seems through my window floating in;
I think I hear from far away
The tunes Dan Harrison used to play.

Dan Harrison — I see him plain,
    Beside the roaring, winter hearth,
Playing away with might and main,
    His honest face aglow with mirth;
And when he laid his bow aside,
"Well done! well done!" he gayly cried;
Well done! well done! indeed were they,
The tunes Dan Harrison used to play.

I do not know what tunes he played,
    I cannot name one melody;
His instrument was never made
    In old Cremona o'er the sea;
And yet I sadly, sadly fear
Such tunes I never more may hear,
Some were so mournful, some so gay,
The tunes Dan Harrison used to play.

I have been witness to the skill
    Of many a master of the bow,
But none has had the power to thrill
    Like him I celebrate; and so

I sit and strive, not all in vain,
To hear his minstrelsy again ;
And from the past I call to-day
The tunes Dan Harrison used to play.

And with the music, as it floats,
   Seraphic harping faintly blends ;
I catch amid the mingling notes
   Familiar voices of old friends ;
And all my pensive soul within
Is melted by the violin,
That yields, at fancy's magic sway,
The tunes Dan Harrison used to play.

THOMAS BAILEY ALDRICH
1836 –

NOCTURNE

UP to her chamber window
   A slight wire trellis goes,
And up this Romeo's ladder
   Clambers a bold white rose.

I lounge in the ilex shadows,
   I see the lady lean,
Unclasping her silken girdle,
   The curtain folds between.

She smiles on her white-rose lover,
   She reaches out her hand
And helps him in at the window —
   I see it where I stand!

To her scarlet lip she holds him,
   And kisses him many a time —
Ah, me! it was he that won her
   Because he dared to climb!

AMONTILLADO

[*In a rhythm of Mr. Thackeray*]

RAFTERS black with smoke,
    White with sand the floor is,
Twenty whiskered Dons
    Calling to Dolores —
Tawny flower of Spain,
    Wild rose of Granada,
Keeper of the wines
    In this old posada.

Hither, light-of-foot,
    Dolores — Juno — Circe !
Pretty Spanish girl
    Without a grain of mercy !
Here I 'm travel-worn,
    Sad, and thirsty very,
And she does not fetch
    The Amontillado sherry !

Thank you, breath of June !
    Now my heart beats free ; ah,
Kisses for your hand,
    Mariquita mia.
You shall live in song,
    Warm and ripe and cheery,
Mellowing with years
    Like Amontillado sherry !

While the earth spins round
    And the stars lean over,
May this amber sprite
    Never lack a lover.

Blessèd be the man
  Who lured her from the berry,
And blest the girl that brings
  The Amontillado sherry!

Sorrow, get thee hence!
  Care, be gone, blue dragon!
Only shapes of joy
  Are sculptured on the flagon.
Kisses — repartees —
  Lyrics — all that 's merry
Rise to touch the lip
  In Amontillado sherry.

Here be wit and mirth,
  And love, the arch enchanter;
Here the golden blood
  Of saints in this decanter.
When pale Charon comes
  To row me o'er his ferry,
I 'll fee him with a case
  Of Amontillado sherry!

What! the flagon 's dry?
  Hark, old Time's confession —
Both hands crossed at XII,
  Owning his transgression!
Pray, old monk, for all
  Generous souls and merry;
May they have their share
  Of Amontillado sherry!

THALIA

I SAY it under the rose —
  Oh, thanks! — yes, under the laurel,
We part lovers, not foes;
  We are not going to quarrel.

We have too long been friends
  On foot and in gilded coaches,
Now that the whole thing ends,
  To spoil our kiss with reproaches.

I leave you; my soul is wrung;
  I pause, look back from the portal —
Ah, I no more am young,
  And you, child, you are immortal!

Mine is the glacier's way,
  Yours is the blossom's weather —
When were December and May
  Known to be happy together?

Before my kisses grow tame,
  Before my moodiness grieve you,
While yet my heart is flame,
  And I all lover, I leave you.

So, in the coming time,
  When you count the rich years over,
Think of me in my prime,
  And not as a white-haired lover,

Fretful, pierced with regret,
   The wraith of a dead Desire
Thrumming a cracked spinet
   By a slowly dying fire.

When, at last, I am cold —
   Years hence, if the gods so will it —
Say, "He was true as gold,"
   And wear a rose in your fillet!

Others, tender as I,
   Will come and sue for caresses,
Woo you, win you, and die —
   Mind you, a rose in your tresses!

Some Melpomene woo,
   Some hold Clio the nearest;
You, sweet Comedy — you
   Were ever sweetest and dearest!

Nay, it is time to go.
   When writing your tragic sister
Say to that child of woe
   How sorry I was I missed her.

Really I cannot stay,
   Though "parting is such sweet sorrow" . . .
Perhaps I will, on my way
   Down-town, look in to-morrow!

IN AN ATELIER

I PRAY you, do not turn your head;
And let your hands lie folded, so.
It was a dress like this, wine-red,
That troubled Dante, long ago.
You don't know Dante? Never mind.
He loved a lady wondrous fair —
His model? Something of the kind.
I wonder if she had your hair!

I wonder if she looked so meek,
And was not meek at all (my dear,
I want that side light on your cheek).
He loved her, it is very clear,
And painted her, as I paint you,
But rather better, on the whole
(Depress your chin; yes, that will do):
He was a painter of the soul!

(And painted portraits, too, I think,
In the Inferno — devilish good!
I 'd make some certain critics blink
Had I his method and his mood.)
Her name was (Fanny, let your glance
Rest there, by that majolica tray) —
Was Beatrice; they met by chance —
They met by chance, the usual way.

(As you and I met, months ago,
Do you remember? How your feet
Went crinkle-crinkle on the snow
Along the bleak gas-lighted street!

An instant in the drug-store's glare
You stood as in a golden frame,
And then I swore it, then and there,
To hand your sweetness down to fame.)

They met, and loved, and never wed
(All this was long before our time,)
And though they died, they are not dead —
Such endless youth gives mortal rhyme!
Still walks the earth, with haughty mien,
Pale Dante, in his soul's distress;
And still the lovely Florentine
Goes lovely in her wine-red dress.

You do not understand at all?
He was a poet; on his page
He drew her; and, though kingdoms fall,
This lady lives from age to age.
A poet — that means painter too,
For words are colors, rightly laid;
And they outlast our brightest hue,
For varnish cracks and crimsons fade.

The poets — they are lucky ones!
When *we* are thrust upon the shelves,
Our works turn into skeletons
Almost as quickly as ourselves;
For our poor canvas peels at length,
At length is prized — when all is bare:
"What grace!" the critics cry, "what strength!"
When neither strength nor grace is there.

Ah, Fanny, I am sick at heart,
It is so little one can do;
We talk our jargon — live for Art!
I'd much prefer to live for you.

How dull and lifeless colors are!
You smile, and all my picture lies:
I wish that I could crush a star
To make a pigment for your eyes.

Yes, child, I know, I'm out of tune;
The light is bad; the sky is gray:
I paint no more this afternoon,
So lay your royal gear away.
Besides, you're moody — chin on hand —
I know not what — not in the vein —
Not like Anne Bullen, sweet and bland:
You sit there smiling in disdain.

Not like the Tudor's radiant Queen,
Unconscious of the coming woe,
But rather as she might have been,
Preparing for the headsman's blow.
So, I have put you in a miff —
Sitting bolt-upright, wrist on wrist.
How *should* you look? Why, dear, as if —
Somehow — as if you'd just been kissed!

L'EAU DORMANTE

CURLED up and sitting on her feet,
　　Within the window's deep embrasure,
Is Lydia; and across the street,
　　A lad, with eyes of roguish azure,
Watches her buried in her book.
In vain he tries to win a look,
And from the trellis over there
Blows sundry kisses through the air,
Which miss the mark, and fall unseen,
Uncared for. Lydia is thirteen.

My lad, if you, without abuse,
　　Will take advice from one who's wiser,
And put his wisdom to more use
　　Than ever yet did your adviser;
If you will let, as none will do,
Another's heartbreak serve for two,
You'll have a care, some four years hence,
How you lounge there by yonder fence
And blow those kisses through that screen —
For Lydia will be seventeen.

ON AN INTAGLIO HEAD OF MINERVA

BENEATH the warrior's helm, behold
  The flowing tresses of the woman!
Minerva, Pallas, what you will —
  A winsome creature, Greek or Roman.

Minerva? No! 't is some sly minx
  In cousin's helmet masquerading;
If not — then Wisdom was a dame
  For sonnets and for serenading!

I thought the goddess cold, austere,
  Not made for love's despairs and blisses:
Did Pallas wear her hair like that?
  Was Wisdom's mouth so shaped for kisses?

The Nightingale should be her bird,
  And not the Owl, big-eyed and solemn:
How very fresh she looks, and yet
  She's older far than Trajan's Column!

The magic hand that carved this face,
  And set this vine-work round it running,
Perhaps ere mighty Phidias wrought
  Had lost its subtle skill and cunning.

Who was he? Was he glad or sad,
  Who knew to carve in such a fashion?
Perchance he graved the dainty head
  For some brown girl that scorned his passion.

Perchance, in some still garden-place,
　　Where neither fount nor tree to-day is,
He flung the jewel at the feet
　　Of Phryne, or perhaps 't was Laïs.

But he is dust; we may not know
　　His happy or unhappy story:
Nameless, and dead these centuries,
　　His work outlives him — there's his glory!

Both man and jewel lay in earth
　　Beneath a lava-buried city;
The countless summers came and went
　　With neither haste, nor hate, nor pity.

Years blotted out the man, but left
　　The jewel fresh as any blossom,
Till some Visconti dug it up —
　　To rise and fall on Mabel's bosom!

O nameless brother! see how Time
　　Your gracious handiwork has guarded:
See how your loving, patient art
　　Has come, at last, to be rewarded.

Who would not suffer slights of men,
　　And pangs of hopeless passion also,
To have his carven agate-stone
　　On such a bosom rise and fall so!

WILLIAM DEAN HOWELLS
1837 –

THE THORN

"Every Rose, you sang, has its Thorn,
    But this has none, I know."
She clasped my rival's Rose
    Over her breast of snow.

I bowed to hide my pain,
    With a man's unskilful art;
I moved my lips, and could not say
    The Thorn was in my heart!

MARY MAPES DODGE
1838 –

THE MINUET

GRANDMA told me all about it,
Told me so I could n't doubt it,
How she danced — my Grandma danced! —
    Long ago.
How she held her pretty head,
How her dainty skirt she spread,
Turning out her little toes;
How she slowly leaned and rose —
    Long ago.

Grandma's hair was bright and sunny;
Dimpled cheeks, too — ah, how funny!
  Really quite a pretty girl,
    Long ago.
Bless her! why, she wears a cap,
Grandma does, and takes a nap
Every single day; and yet
Grandma danced the minuet
    Long ago.

Now she sits there rocking, rocking,
Always knitting Grandpa's stocking —
  (Every girl was taught to knit
    Long ago.)

Yet her figure is so neat,
And her ways so staid and sweet,
I can almost see her now
Bending to her partner's bow,
      Long ago.

Grandma says our modern jumping,
Hopping, rushing, whirling, bumping,
  Would have shocked the gentle folk
      Long ago.
No — they moved with stately grace,
Everything in proper place,
Gliding slowly forward, then
Slowly curtesying back again,
      Long ago.

Modern ways are quite alarming,
Grandma says; but boys were charming —
  Girls and boys I mean, of course —
      Long ago.
Bravely modest, grandly shy, —
She would like to have us try
Just to feel like those who met
In the graceful minuet
      Long ago.

With the minuet in fashion,
Who could fly into a passion?
  All would wear the calm they wore
      Long ago.
In time to come, if I, perchance,
Should tell my grandchild of *our* dance,
I should really like to say,
"We did it, dear, in some such way,
      Long ago."

OVER THE WAY

OVER the way, over the way,
 I 've seen a head that 's fair and gray;
I 've seen kind eyes not new to tears,
A form of grace, though full of years.
 Her fifty summers have left no flaw —
And I, a youth of twenty-three,
So love this lady, fair to see,
 I want her for my mother-in-law!

Over the way, over the way,
I 've seen her with the children play;
I 've seen her with a royal grace
Before the mirror adjust her lace;
 A kinder woman none ever saw;
God bless and cheer her onward path,
And bless all treasures that she hath,
 And let her be my mother-in-law!

Over the way, over the way,
I think I 'll venture, dear, some day
(If you will lend a helping hand,
And sanctify the scheme I 've planned),
 I 'll kneel in loving, reverent awe,
Down at the lady's feet, and say:
"I 've loved your daughter many a day —
 Please won't you be my mother-in-law?"

LITTLE WORDS

How wise he is! He can talk in Greek!
There is n't a language he cannot speak.
The very measure the Psalmist sung
He carries at will on the tip of his tongue.
When he argues in English, why, every word
Is almost the biggest that ever you heard!
That is, when he talks with Papa it 's so —
With me it 's another affair, you know.

Little one-syllable words, you see,
Are all he is willing to waste upon me;
So he calls me his rose, his bird, his pet,
And says it quite often, lest I should forget;
While his wonderful verbs grow meagre and small;
You 'd think he had ne'er opened Webster at all.
It 's only: "Ah, do you?" or "Will you, my dove?"
Or else it 's: "I love," "I love," and "I love."

And when we walk out in the starry night,
Though he knows the Zodiac's rounded height,
With its Gemini, Scorpio, Leo, and all,
Its nebulæ, planets, and satellites small,
And though, in a flash, he could turn his proud eye on
The Dipper, and Crown, and the Belt of Orion; —
Not once does he mention the wonders above,
But just whispers softly: "My own!" and "I love!"

Whenever they tease me — the girls and boys —
With: "Mrs. Professor," or "classical joys;"
Or ask if his passion he deigns to speak
In Hebrew, or Sanscrit or simple Greek; —

I try to summon a look of steel,
And hide the joy that I really feel.
For they 'd laugh still more if they knew the truth
How meek a professor can be, forsooth !

Though well I know, in the days to come
Great thoughts shall preside in our happy home ;
And to hold forever his loving looks
I must bend my head over musty books,
And be as learned as ever I can
To do full justice to such a man, —
The future is bright, for, like song of birds,
My soul is filled with his little words.

JOHN HAY
1838 –

HOW IT HAPPENED

I PRAY you, pardon me, Elsie,
   And smile that frown away
That dims the light of your lovely face
   As a thunder-cloud the day.
I really could not help it, —
   Before I thought, 't was done, —
And those great gray eyes flashed bright and cold,
   Like an icicle in the sun.

I was thinking of the summers
   When we were boys and girls,
And wandered in the blossoming woods,
   And the gay winds romped with your curls.
And you seemed to me the same little girl
   I kissed in the alder-path,
I kissed the little girl's lips, and alas!
   I have roused a woman's wrath.

There is not so much to pardon, —
   For why were your lips so red?
The blond hair fell in a shower of gold
   From the proud, provoking head.
And the beauty that flashed from the splendid eyes,
   And played round the tender mouth,
Rushed over my soul like a warm sweet wind
   That blows from the fragrant south.

And where, after all, is the harm done?
    I believe we were made to be gay,
And all of youth not given to love
    Is vainly squandered away.
And strewn through life's low labors,
    Like gold in the desert sands,
Are love's swift kisses and sighs and vows
    And the clasp of clinging hands.

And when you are old and lonely,
    In Memory's magic shrine
You will see on your thin and wasting hands,
    Like gems, these kisses of mine.
And when you muse at evening
    At the sound of some vanished name,
The ghost of my kisses shall touch your lips
    And kindle your heart to flame.

BRET HARTE

1839 – 1902

MISS BLANCHE SAYS

AND you are the poet, and so you want
   Something — what is it? — a theme, a fancy?
Something or other the Muse won't grant
   In your old poetical necromancy;
Why one half your poets — you can't deny —
   Don't know the Muse when you chance to meet her,
But sit in your attics and mope and sigh
For a faineant goddess to drop from the sky,
When flesh and blood may be standing by
   Quite at your service, should you but greet her.

What if I told you my own romance?
   Women are poets, if you so take them,
One-third poet — the rest what chance
   Of man and marriage may choose to make them.
Give me ten minutes before you go, —
   Here at the window we'll sit together,
Watching the currents that ebb and flow;
Watching the world as it drifts below
Up to the hot Avenue's dusty glow:
   Is n't it pleasant — this bright June weather?

Well, it was after the war broke out,
   And I was a school-girl fresh from Paris;
Papa had contracts, and roamed about,
   And I — did nothing — for I was an heiress.

Picked some lint, now I think ; perhaps
    Knitted some stockings — a dozen nearly ;
Havelocks made for the soldiers' caps ;
Stood at fair tables and peddled traps
Quite at a profit. The " shoulder-straps "
    Thought I was pretty. Ah, thank you ! really?

Still it was stupid. Rata-tat-tat !
    Those were the sounds of that battle summer,
Till the earth seemed a parchment round and flat,
    And every footfall the tap of a drummer ;
And day by day down the Avenue went
    Cavalry, infantry, all together,
Till my pitying angel one day sent
My fate in the shape of a regiment,
That halted, just as the day was spent,
    Here at our door in the bright June weather.

None of your dandy warriors they,
    Men from the West, but where I know not ;
Haggard and travel-stained, worn and grey,
    With never a ribbon or lace or bow-knot :
And I opened the window, and leaning there,
    I felt in their presence the free winds blowing ;
My neck and shoulders and arms were bare —
I did not dream they might think me fair,
But I had some flowers that night in my hair,
    And here on my bosom, a red rose glowing.

And I looked from the window along the line,
    Dusty and dirty and grim and solemn,
Till an eye like a bayonet flash met mine,
    And a dark face grew from the darkening column,
And a quick flame leaped to my eyes and hair,
    Till cheeks and shoulders burned all together,
And the next I found myself standing there
With my eyelids wet and my cheeks less fair,
And the rose from my bosom tossed high in air,
    Like a blood-drop falling on plume and feather.

Then I drew back quickly: there came a cheer,
    A rush of figures, a noise and tussle,
And then it was over, and high and clear
    My red rose bloomed on his gun's black muzzle.
Then far in the darkness a sharp voice cried,
    And slowly and steadily, all together,
Shoulder to shoulder and side to side,
Rising and falling, and swaying wide,
But bearing above them the rose, my pride,
    They marched away in the twilight weather.

And I leaned from my window and watched my rose
    Tossed on the waves of the surging column,
Warmed from above in the sunset glows,
    Borne from below by an impulse solemn.
Then I shut the window. I heard no more
    Of my soldier friend, my flower neither,
But lived my life as I did before.
I did not go as a nurse to the war —
Sick folks to me are a dreadful bore —
    So I didn't go to the hospital either.

You smile, O poet, and what do you?
    You lean from your window, and watch life's column
Trampling and struggling through dust and dew,
    Filled with its purposes grave and solemn;
An act, a gesture, a face — who knows?
    Touches your fancy to thrill and haunt you,
And you pluck from your bosom the verse that grows,
And down it flies like my red, red rose,
And you sit and dream as away it goes,
    And think that your duty is done — now don't you?

I know your answer. I'm not yet through.
    Look at this photograph — "In the Trenches!"
That dead man in the coat of blue
    Holds a withered rose in his hand. That clenches

Nothing! — except that the sun paints true,
  And a woman is sometimes prophetic-minded.
And that's my romance. And, poet, you
Take it and mould it to suit your view;
And who knows but you may find it too
  Come to your heart once more, as mine did.

HER LETTER

I'M sitting alone by the fire,
  Dressed just as I came from the dance,
In a robe even *you* would admire, —
  It cost a cool thousand in France;
I'm be-diamonded out of all reason,
  My hair is done up in a cue:
In short, sir, "the belle of the season"
  Is wasting an hour on you.

A dozen engagements I've broken;
  I left in the midst of a set;
Likewise a proposal, half spoken,
  That waits — on the stairs — for me yet.
They say he'll be rich, — when he grows up, —
  And then he adores me indeed.
And you, sir, are turning your nose up,
  Three thousand miles off as you read.

"And how do I like my position?"
  "And what do I think of New York?"
"And now, in my higher ambition,
  With whom do I waltz, flirt, or talk?"
"And is n't it nice to have riches,
  And diamonds and silks, and all that?"
"And are n't they a change to the ditches
  And tunnels of Poverty Flat?"

Well, yes, — if you saw us out driving
  Each day in the park, four-in-hand, —
If you saw poor dear mamma contriving
  To look supernaturally grand, —

If you saw papa's picture, as taken
  By Brady, and tinted at that, —
You 'd never suspect he sold bacon
  And flour at Poverty Flat.

And yet, just this moment, when sitting
  In the glare of the grand chandelier, —
In the bustle and glitter befitting
  The " finest *soirée* of the year," —
In the mists of a *gauze de Chambéry*,
  And the hum of the smallest of talk, —
Somehow, Joe, I thought of the " Ferry,"
  And the dance that we had on " The Fork ; "

Of Harrison's barn, with its muster
  Of flags festooned over the wall ;
Of the candles that shed their soft lustre
  And tallow on head-dress and shawl ;
Of the steps that we took to one fiddle ;
  Of the dress of my queer *vis-à-vis* ;
And how I once went down the middle
  With the man that shot Sandy McGee ;

Of the moon that was quietly sleeping
  On the hill when the time came to go ;
Of the few baby peaks that were peeping
  From under their bed-clothes of snow ;
Of that ride, — that to me was the rarest ;
  Of — the something you said at the gate, —
Ah, Joe, then I was n't an heiress
  To " the best-paying lead in the State."

Well, well, it's all past ; yet it's funny
  To think, as I stood in the glare
Of fashion and beauty and money,
  That I should be thinking, right there,

Of some one who breasted high water,
   And swam the North Fork, and all that,
Just to dance with old Folinsbee's daughter,
   The Lily of Poverty Flat.

But goodness! what nonsense I'm writing!
   (Mamma says my taste still is low,)
Instead of my triumphs reciting,
   I'm spooning on Joseph, — heigh-ho!
And I'm to be "finished" by travel, —
   Whatever's the meaning of that, —
Oh! why did papa strike pay gravel
   In drifting on Poverty Flat?

Good night, — here's the end of my paper;
   Good night, — if the longitude please, —
For may be, while wasting my taper,
   Your sun's climbing over the trees.
But know, if you haven't got riches,
   And are poor, dearest Joe, and all that,
That my heart's somewhere there in the ditches,
   And you've struck it, — on Poverty Flat.

DOLLY VARDEN

DEAR Dolly! who does not recall
  The thrilling page that pictured all
Those charms that held our sense in thrall.
  Just as the artist caught her —
As down that English lane she tripped,
In bowered chintz, hat sideways tipped,
Trim-bodiced, bright-eyed, roguish-lipped,
  The locksmith's pretty daughter?

Sweet fragment of the Master's art!
O simple faith! O rustic heart!
O maid that hath no counterpart
  In life's dry, dog-eared pages!
Where shall we find thy like? Ah, stay!
Methinks I saw her yesterday
In chintz that flowered, as one might say,
  Perennial for ages.

Her father's modest cot was stone,
Five stories high; in style and tone
Composite, and, I frankly own,
  Within its walls revealing
Some certain novel, strange ideas:
A Gothic door with Roman piers,
And floors removed some thousand years
  From their Pompeian ceiling.

The small salon where she received
Was Louis Quatorze, and relieved
By Chinese cabinets, conceived
  Grotesquely by the heathen;

The sofas were a classic sight —
The Roman bench (sedilia hight);
The chairs were French in gold and white,
  And one Elizabethan.

And she, the goddess of that shrine,
Two ringed fingers placed in mine —
The stones were many carats fine,
  And of the purest water —
Then dropped a curtsey, far enough
To fairly fill her cretonne puff
And show the petticoat's rich stuff
  That her fond parent bought her.

Her speech was simple as her dress —
Not French the more, but English less,
She loved; yet sometimes, I confess,
  I scarce could comprehend her.
Her manners were quite far from shy:
There was a quiet in her eye
Appalling to the Hugh who'd try
  With rudeness to offend her.

"But whence," I cried, "this masquerade?
Some figure for to-night's charade —
A Watteau shepherdess or maid?"
  She smiled and begged my pardon:
"Why, surely you must know the name —
That woman who was Shakespeare's flame
Or Byron's —well, it's all the same:
  Why, Lord! I'm Dolly Varden!"

WHAT THE WOLF REALLY SAID TO LITTLE RED RIDING-HOOD

WONDERING maiden, so puzzled and fair,
    Why dost thou murmur and ponder and stare?
"Why are my eyelids so open and wild?" —
Only the better to see with, my child!
Only the better and clearer to view
Cheeks that are rosy and eyes that are blue.

Dost thou still wonder, and ask why these arms
Fill thy soft bosom with tender alarms,
Swaying so wickedly? — are they misplaced
Clasping or shielding some delicate waist:
Hands whose coarse sinews may fill you with fear
Only the better protect you, my dear!

Little Red Riding-Hood, when in the street,
Why do I press your small hand when we meet?
Why, when you timidly offered your cheek,
Why did I sigh, and why did n't I speak?
Why, well: you see — if the truth must appear —
I 'm not your grandmother, Riding-Hood, dear!

AMELIA WALSTEIN CARPENTER
1840 –

OLD FLEMISH LACE

ALONG, rich breadth of Holland lace,
   A window by a Flemish sea;
Huge men go by with mighty pace, —
Great Anne was Queen these days, may be,
And strange ships prowled for spoil the sea —
      For you — old lace!

Stitch after stitch enwrought with grace,
   The mist falls cold on Zuyder-Zee;
The silver tankards hang in place
Along the wall; across her knee
Dame Snuyder spreads her square of lace,
      A veil — for me?

The Holland dames put by their lace,
   The bells of Bruges ring out in glee;
The mill-wheels move in sluggish race: —
   Farewell, sweet bells! Then down the sea
The slow ship brings the bridal grace —
      The veil — for me!

Manhattan shores — a New World place,
   The Pinxter-blows their sweetest be:
And now — come close, O love-bright face —
   Bend low — . . .
          Nay, not old Trinity,
To Olde Sainte Marke's i' the Bowerie,
      Dear Hal, — with thee!

NORA PERRY
1841 - 1896

SWEET SIXTEEN

"YOU think the world is only made
    For you, and such as you," he said,
Laughing aloud in boyish scorn,
Of boyish mirth and mischief born.

She never turned from where she stood
Prinking her little silken snood
Of silken curls before the glass;
She never turned to see him pass.

Nor answered him, save with a laugh
That half confessed his boyish " chaff."
But left alone, confronted there,
With her own image fresh and fair.

A sudden blush lit up her face
With newer youth and fresher grace,
And eyes that were demurely fixed
A moment since, with thought unmixed,

Upon the smoothing of a tress,
Now sparkled soft with consciousness.
" Why not, why not?" she lightly cried,
Out of the gay, exultant pride,

The sweet, wild innocence of youth;
"Why not for me, for me, forsooth,
And such as me, the world be made;
For me its glories all arrayed?

"For since the world and life begun,
What poet's measures have not run
Through all the strains of minstrelsy
In praise of me, and such as me?

"For youth and beauty, in its day,
Has ruled the world, and will for aye,
One greatest of them all has sung
In verse that through the world has rung.

"And here's my days to live and reign,
To take the joy and leave the pain
From this old world that's made for me,
For me, for me, and such as me!"

Gay laughter rang through every word,
And yet beneath the laughter stirred
A something more than jesting play —
Just sweet sixteen that very day.

She half believed, in sober truth,
In the sweet insolence of youth,
That all for her — a foolish maid —
The world's gay glories were arrayed.

THE LOVE-KNOT

TYING her bonnet under her chin,
    She tied her raven ringlets in;
But not alone in the silken snare
Did she catch her lovely floating hair,
For, tying her bonnet under her chin,
She tied a young man's heart within.

They were strolling together up the hill,
Where the wind comes blowing merry and chill;
And it blew the curls, a frolicsome race,
All over the happy peach-colored face,
Till, scolding and laughing, she tied them in,
Under her beautiful dimpled chin.

And it blew a color, bright as the bloom
Of the pinkest fuchsia's tossing plume,
All over the cheeks of the prettiest girl
That ever imprisoned a romping curl,
Or, tying her bonnet under her chin,
Tied a young man's heart within.

Steeper and steeper grew the hill;
Madder, merrier, chillier still
The western wind blew down, and played
The wildest tricks with the little maid,
As, tying her bonnet under her chin,
She tied a young man's heart within.

O western wind, do you think it was fair
To play such tricks with her floating hair?
To gladly, gleefully do your best
To blow her against the young man's breast,

Where he as gladly folded her in,
And kissed her mouth and her dimpled chin?

Ah! Ellery Vane, you little thought,
An hour ago, when you besought
This country lass to walk with you,
After the sun had dried the dew,
What perilous danger you 'd be in,
As she tied her bonnet under her chin!

YESTERDAY

WHAT if but yesterday
  I laughed and said him nay,
When here's to-day, to-day
To change my mind and say
A sweeter word than nay.

What if but yesterday
I told him that my nay
Could never turn to yea,
Though he should pray and pray
Forever and a day.

What if but yesterday
He swore he would obey
My cruel will, nor stay
To further sue or pray, —
Then strode in wrath away.

What if but yesterday
Like this he strode away,
When here's to-day, to-day
For him to hear me say, —
" I love you, Love, to-day! "

FREDERICK WADSWORTH LORING
1848–1871

THE OLD PROFESSOR

THE old professor taught no more,
    But lingered round the college walks; —
Stories of him we boys told o'er,
    Before the fire, in evening talks.
I 'll ne'er forget how he came in
    To recitation, one March night,
And asked our tutor to begin,
    " And let me hear these boys recite."

As we passed out, we heard him say,
    " Pray leave me here a while, alone.
Here in my old place let me stay
    Just as I did in years long flown."
Our tutor smiled and bowed consent,
    Rose courteous from his high-backed chair,
And down the darkening stairs he went,
    Leaving the old professor there.

The lecture room was dark and bare,
    The old professor sat alone :
The bust of Virgil seemed to stare
    Upon him with its eyes of stone.
The lights shone here and there, outside ;
    The last class down the stairs had rushed ;
Stillness spread through the entries wide,
    In every room all noise was hushed.

From out the shadows faces seemed
    To look on him in his old place, —
Fresh faces that with radiance beamed,
    Radiance of boyish hope and grace ;
And faces that had lost their youth,
    Although in years they still were young ;
And faces o'er whose love and truth
    The funeral anthem had been sung.

"These are my boys," he murmured then,
    "My boys, as in the years long past ;
Though some are angels, others men,
    Still as my boys I hold them fast.
There 's one don't know his lesson now,
    That one of me is making fun,
And that one 's cheating : — ah ! I see,
    I see and love them every one.

"And is it then so long ago
    This chapter in my life was told,
Did all of them thus come and go,
    And have I really grown so old?
No ! here are my old pains and joys,
    My book once more is in my hand,
Once more I hear these very boys,
    And seek their hearts to understand."
    .   .   .   .
They found him there with open book,
    And eyes closed with a calm content ;
The same old sweetness in his look
    There used to be when fellows went
To ask him questions and to talk,
    When recitations were all o'er ; —
We saw him in the college walk
    And in his former place no more.

December 10, 1869

EDWARD ROWLAND SILL
1841–1887

EVE'S DAUGHTER

I WAITED in the little sunny room:
  The cool breeze waved the window-lace, at play,
The white rose on the porch was all in bloom,
    And out upon the bay
I watched the wheeling sea-birds go and come.
"Such an old friend, — she would not make me stay
While she bound up her hair." I turned, and lo,
Danaë in her shower! and fit to slay
    All a man's hoarded prudence at a blow:
Gold hair that streamed away
As round some nymph a sunlit fountain's flow.
"She would not make me wait!" — but well I know
She took a good half-hour to loose and lay
Those locks in dazzling disarrangement so!

ANNIE DOUGLAS ROBINSON

[MARIAN DOUGLAS]

1842

PICTURE POEMS FOR YOUNG FOLKS

"IS the yellow bird dead?
    Lay your dear little head
Close, close to my heart, and weep, precious one, there:
   "While your beautiful hair
On my bosom lies light, like a sun-lighted cloud:
    No, you need not keep still,
    You may sob as you will;
There is some little comfort in crying aloud.

    "But the days they must come
    When your grief will be dumb:
Grown women, like me, must take care how they cry,
    You will learn, by-and-bye;
'T is a womanly art to hide pain out of sight,
    To look round with a smile,
    Tho' your heart aches the while,
And to keep back your tears till you 've blown out the light."

MARC COOK

[VANDYKE BROWN]

1854–1882

AN HONEST CONFESSION

WITH thoughts of companionship only,
   I sit in my bleak little room,
Dejected, despondent, and lonely,
   While the twilight deepens to gloom;
I sit here and stare at the ceiling,
   And muse and wonder and think
How hard is the task of living
   By paper and pen and ink.

Ah, once, I remember, I fancied
   That writing would win me a name —
The world at that time seemed fairer,
   And I yearned for the bubble of fame:
So, filled with a burning desire,
   I sat down to labor and think —
To astonish mankind by the magic
   Of paper and pen and ink.

I began on an epic, and finished
   Some twenty odd lines, and no more;
Then essayed, with pluck undiminished,
   A drama, which died at Act Four;

Then I courted the coy Erato,
  Nor permitted my spirits to sink —
I was bound to get riches and honor
  From paper and pen and ink.

Alas for the dreams that I cherished
  When first I laid hold of a pen!
Alas for the hopes that have perished,
  And the misery suffered since then!
Where now is that spirit courageous
  Which was never to falter or shrink?
Where — where are the triumphs I dreamed of
  With paper and pen and ink?

Once it caused me a thrill and a flutter
  To see my effusions in print;
Now I write for my bread and my butter,
  And my heart is hard as a flint;
You may talk of the mythical muses,
  But the craving for meat and for drink
Is the truest incentive to labor
  With paper and pen and ink!

I weave the most thrilling romances
  Out of fabrics exceedingly thin —
Brave knights with their armor and lances,
  And maidens with lily-white skin;
And I murder those maidens so lovely,
  Then restore 'em to life in a wink.
And marry 'em off to a villain,
  With paper and pen and ink!

I have won neither wealth nor position,
  Nor the coveted prize of a name;
I have buried the dreams of ambition,
  And forgotten the phantom of fame.

I labor no longer on epics,
    Nor tremble on tragedy's brink —
I 'm thankful to earn a bare living
    With paper and pen and ink.

So, with thoughts of companionship only
    I sit in my bleak little room,
Dejected, despondent, and lonely,
    While the twilight deepens with gloom;
I sit here and stare at the ceiling,
    And smile to myself as I think
Of the castles in Spain I erected
    On paper and pen and ink.

MARC COOK

GROWING OLD

AT six — I well remember when —
I fancied all folks old at ten.

But when I 'd turned my first decade,
Fifteen appeared more truly staid.

But when the fifteenth round I 'd run,
I thought none old till twenty-one.

Then oddly, when I 'd reached that age,
I held that thirty made folks sage.

But when my thirtieth year was told,
I said: "At twoscore men grow old!"

Yet twoscore came and found me thrifty,
And so I drew the line at fifty.

But when I reached that age, I swore
None could be old until threescore!

And here I am at sixty now,
As young as when at six, I trow!

'T is true, my hair is somewhat gray,
And that I use a cane, to-day;

'T is true these rogues about my knee
Say "Grandpa!" when they speak to me;

But, bless your soul, I 'm young as when
I thought all people old at ten!

Perhaps a little wiser grown —
Perhaps some old illusions flown;

But wond'ring still, while years have rolled,
When is it that a man grows old?

HER OPINION OF THE PLAY

DO I like it? I think it just splendid!
   You see how I speak out my mind,
And I think 't would be better if men did
   The same when they feel so inclined.
But no, you 're all dumb as an oyster,
   You critics who sit here and stare,
Looking grave as a monk in his cloister —
   You have n't laughed once, I declare!

I 'm sure there 's been lots that is jolly,
   And more that 's exciting, you 'll own;
Why, I pity the poor hero's folly
   As if he were some one I 'd known!
And was n't it grand and heroic
   When he shielded that friendless girl Sue?
'T would have quickened the pulse of a stoic,
   But of course, sir, it could n't rouse you!

And then for the villain De Lancey —
   Now, does n't he act with a dash?
Such art and such delicate fancy,
   And — did you observe his moustache?
He made my very blood tingle
   When he threw himself down on his knees —
Do you know if he 's married or single?
   Yes, the villain — there, laugh if you please!

I admit I know nothing of "action,"
   Of "unities," "plot," and the rest,
But the play gives complete satisfaction,
   And that is a good enough test.

Yes, I know you will pick it to pieces
   In your horribly savage review,
But, for me, its interest increases
   Because 't will be censured by you!

I should think 't would be awfully jolly
   For the author to make such a hit;
How he pricks all the bubbles of folly
   With his sharp little needle of wit!
I am sure he is perfectly charming,
   Or he never could write such a play —
(I declare, sir, it 's really alarming
   To have you sit staring that way!)

And oh, if I only were brighter,
   And not such a poor little dunce,
I should so like to meet with the writer,
   For I know I should love him at once.
Yes, I should, though you think it audacious,
   And I 'd tell him so, too, which is more,
And — *you* are the author? — good gracious!
   Why did n't you say so before?

TO A PRETTY SCHOOLMA'AM

IF only fate would grant, thus late, the one thing I beseech 'er —
That I might go to school again, and have you for my teacher —
I'd pick up more of solid lore before a week was ended
Than ever yet I've chanced to get at all the schools I've 'tended.

I wouldn't ask again to bask in childhood's sunlight brisker —
I'd take my seat just as I am, with coat-tail and with whisker,
And every rule laid down in school should have my strict alliance;
I'd fairly live on wisdom's bread, and drink of naught but science!

The irksome path which learning hath would turn to one of pleasure,
And every musty "ology" become a precious treasure;
With porous mind, intent to find the truth of your instruction,
I'd grow a sort of learned sponge — a philosophic suction!

Astronomy would have for me a charm before unheeded,
When neither chart nor telescope would ever once be needed;
I'd never pore long hours o'er a problem wrong to right it,
For I would make your face the sky, your eyes the stars that light it.

For botany I'd quickly cull the very germ and essence,
And learn to tell the *panicle* or *spadix inflorescence*.
Ah, little need I'd have indeed of what the book deposes;
I'd take your cheeks for specimens, and analyze their roses.

Conchology would no more be a science dull and prosy;
I'd catch a sight of small teeth white between lips ripe and rosy,
And then for bivalves I would crave, and wonder late and early
If ever in a mollusk yet were hidden pearls so pearly.

And as for ornithology — the cuckoo, *C. canorus*,
Might chirp away the live-long day, I should n't heed his chorus;
Your voice would be enough for me, and with its music ringing,
I'd cease to think the bobolink knew anything of singing.

Mythology would cease to be an antiquated fable,
When I could turn, and there discern a Hebe at the table.
Things palaeontological would live beneath your teaching —
I'd even take theology, if you would do the preaching.

And thus together while we trod through learning's tangled mazes,
And caught a peep at science deep amid its countless phases,
We'd learn at last by physics' laws, most rigidly enacted,
How very natural it is that bodies are attracted!

GEORGE WASHINGTON CABLE
1844 –

AN EDITOR'S FIRST-BORN

THERE came to port, last Sunday night,
  The queerest little craft,
Without an inch of rigging on:
  I looked, and looked, and laughed.

It seemed so curious that she
  Should cross the Unknown water
And moor herself right in my room,
  My daughter, O my daughter!

She has no manifest but this,
  No flag floats o'er the water,
She's too new for the British Lloyds —
  My daughter, O my daughter!

Ring out, wild bells, and tame ones too!
  Ring out the lover's moon!
Ring in the little worsted socks!
  Ring in the bib and spoon!

Ring out the muse! ring in the nurse!
  Ring in the milk and water!
Away with paper, pen, and ink —
  My daughter, O my daughter!

RICHARD WATSON GILDER
1844 –

A MIDSUMMER SONG

OH, father's gone to market-town, he was up before the day,
And Jamie's after robins, and the man is making hay,
And whistling down the hollow goes the boy that minds the mill,
While mother from the kitchen-door is calling with a will,
  "Polly! — Polly! — The cows are in the corn!
    Oh, where's Polly?"

From all the misty morning air there comes a summer sound, —
A murmur as of waters from skies and trees and ground.
The birds they sing upon the wing, the pigeons bill and coo,
And over hill and hollow rings again the loud halloo:
  "Polly! — Polly! — The cows are in the corn!
    Oh, where's Polly?"

Above the trees the honey-bees swarm by with buzz and boom,
And in the field and garden a thousand blossoms bloom.
Within the farmer's meadow a brown-eyed daisy blows,
And down at the edge of the hollow a red and thorny rose.
  But Polly! — Polly! — The cows are in the corn!
    Oh, where's Polly?

How strange at such a time of day the mill should stop its clatter!
The farmer's wife is listening now and wonders what's the matter.
Oh, wild the birds are singing in the wood and on the hill,
While whistling up the hollow goes the boy that minds the mill.
    But Polly! — Polly! — The cows are in the corn!
        Oh, where's Polly?

THEODORE PEASE COOK

1844 –

BLUE–BEARD

HE is not dead, for I am he!
   Nay, little one, you need not start;
   That awful closet is my heart,
I pray you not to turn the key.

You hold the matter in suspense,
   You hesitate, ah! all is lost;
   The key is turned, the threshold crossed,
Now you must take the consequence.

Seven dead loves you bring to view —
   No wonder that you stood aghast;
   You should not dive into the past
If you would trust that men are true.

Seven dead loves! a heavy load.
   You see the first, a little girl
   With violet eyes and teeth of pearl;
That was a school-boy episode.

When college days gave life a glow,
   And tender hearts wrought rapid slaughter,
   I courted the Professor's daughter;
That's she — the second in the row.

I scarcely know how it occurred;
　I spent vacation with a friend,
　And ere three weeks were at an end
I loved his sister — she's the third.

A grim old lawyer taught me Kent;
　I made his mansion my abode,
　And spoke some words not in the "Code" —
His youngest girl knew what they meant.

When Fashion's flame was all alive,
　Where Pleasure flung her golden haze
　Athwart the pathway of the days,
I met and worshipped Number Five.

But yonder, where the maple-tree
　Casts shadows on the old stone wall,
　And slumberous peace broods over all,
A village maid enraptured me.

You see one other figure stand,
　Her memory will forever last;
　I hold her sacred since she passed
The portals of the Silent Land.

So Blue-Beard lives, and I am he:
　But come, Fatima, close the door,
　You cannot love me any more;
The blood of knowledge stains the key.

JOHN BOYLE O'REILLY
1844 – 1890

A WHITE ROSE

THE red rose whispers of passion,
    And the white rose breathes of love;
Oh, the red rose is a falcon,
    And the white rose is a dove.

But I send you a cream-white rosebud
    With a flush on its petal tips;
For the love that is purest and sweetest
    Has a kiss of desire on the lips.

AN ART MASTER

HE gathered cherry-stones, and carved them quaintly
   Into fine semblances of flies and flowers;
With subtle skill, he even imaged faintly
   The forms of tiny maids and ivied towers.

His little blocks he loved to file and polish;
   And ampler means he asked not, but despised.
All art but cherry-stones he would abolish,
   For then his genius would be rightly prized.

For such rude hands as dealt with wrongs and passions,
   And throbbing hearts, he had a pitying smile;
Serene his way through surging years and fashions,
   While Heaven gave him his cherry-stones and file!

HENRY AUGUSTIN BEERS
1847 –

A SHADES

A SHADES there is unknown to fame,
   A shades indeed that very few know,
And fewer still can spell the name
   That decks its windows — Madame Grunot.

(I know a quote here rather pat:
   Perhaps it would n't come amiss,
By Jove, I 'll sling it! here goes; *Stat —*
   Stat umbra magni nominis.)

What 's in a name? The rose *is* sweet,
   Its bower is snug, albeit shady;
The ale is nice, the room is neat,
   And neater still the nice Old Lady.

If Bacchus' self should step in here,
   He 'd hardly miss the rosy Hebe
While smiling Madame pours his beer,
   Or honest Tom or pretty Phebe.

He 'd hardly miss his nectar-cup;
   I 'll bet a fig that every night he
Would here on savory rabbits sup,
   And swig his ale, *sub arta vite.*

JAMES JEFFREY ROCHE
1847–

THE V–A–S–E

FROM the madding crowd they stand apart,
The maidens four and the Work of Art;

And none might tell from sight alone
In which had culture ripest grown, —

The Gotham Millions fair to see,
The Philadelphia Pedigree,

The Boston mind of azure hue,
Or the Soulful Soul from Kalamazoo, —

For all loved Art in a seemly way,
With an earnest soul and a capital A.

. . . .

Long they worshipped; but no one broke
The sacred stillness, until up spoke

The Western one from the nameless place,
Who blushing said, "What a lovely vace!"

Over three faces a sad smile flew,
And they edged away from Kalamazoo.

But Gotham's haughty soul was stirred
To crush the stranger with one small word;

Deftly hiding reproof in praise,
She cries, " 'T is, indeed, a lovely vaze!"

But brief her unworthy triumph when
The lofty one from the home of Penn,

With the consciousness of two grandpapas,
Exclaims, "It is quite a lovely vahs!"

And glances round with an anxious thrill,
Awaiting the word of Beacon Hill.

But the Boston maid smiles courteouslee,
And gently murmurs, "Oh, pardon me!

"I did not catch your remark, because
I was so entranced with that charming vaws!"

>Dies erit praegelida
>Sinistra quum Bostonia.

WALTER LEARNED

1847 –

EHEU! FUGACES

SWEET sixteen is shy and cold,
Calls me "sir," and thinks me old;
Hears in an embarrassed way
All the compliments I pay;

Finds my homage quite a bore,
Will not smile on me, and more
To her taste she finds the noise
And the chat of callow boys.

Not the lines around my eye,
Deepening as the years go by;
Not white hairs that strew my head,
Nor my less elastic tread;

Cares I find, nor joys I miss,
Make me feel my years like this: —
Sweet sixteen is shy and cold,
Calls me " sir," and thinks me old.

CUPID'S KISS

'TWAS as she slept that Cupid came,
　　His bow and arrows taking,
That she might feel his power in dreams
Who scorned his weapons waking.

As o'er her sleeping form he poised
The shaft that oft had missed her,
Her beauty touched his roguish heart —
He only stooped and kissed her.

Since when, upon her fair, soft cheek,
Love's amorous imprint keeping,
A charming dimple marks the place
Where Cupid kissed her, sleeping.

TO CRITICS

WHEN I was seventeen I heard
    From each censorious tongue,
"I'd not do that if I were you;
    You see you're rather young."

Now that I number forty years,
    I'm quite as often told
Of this or that I should n't do
    Because I'm quite too old.

O carping world! If there's an age
    Where youth and manhood keep
An equal poise, alas! I must
    Have passed it in my sleep.

TIME'S REVENGE

WHEN I was ten and she fifteen —
  Ah, me! how fair I thought her.
She treated with disdainful mien
  The homage that I brought her,
And, in a patronizing way,
Would of my shy advances say:
  "It's really quite absurd, you see;
  He's very much too young for me."

I'm twenty now, she twenty-five —
  Well, well! how old she's growing.
I fancy that my suit might thrive
  If pressed again; but, owing
To great discrepancy in age,
Her marked attentions don't engage
  My young affections, for, you see,
  She's really quite too old for me.

FRANCIS SALTUS SALTUS

1849 – 1889

PASTEL

AMONG the priceless gems and treasures rare
   Old Versailles shelters in its halls sublime,
I can recall one faded image fair,
A girl's sad face, praised once in every clime.
Poets have sung, in rich and happy rhyme,
Her violet eyes, the wonder of her hair.
An art-bijou it was, but dimmed by time,
A dreamy pastel of La Vallière !
I, too, remember in my heart a face
Whose charm I deemed would ever with me dwell ;
But as the days went by, its peerless grace
Fled like those dreams that blooming dawn dispel,
Till of its beauty there was left no trace,
Time having blurred it like that pale pastel !

GEORGE A. BAKER
1849 –

"LE DERNIER JOUR D'UN CONDAMNÉ"

OLD coat, for some three or four seasons
  We've been jolly comrades, but now
We part, old companion, forever;
  To fate, and the fashion, I bow.
You'd look well enough at a dinner,
  I'd wear you with pride at a ball,
But I'm dressing to-night for a wedding —
  My own, and you'd not do at all.

You've too many wine-stains about you,
  You're scented too much with cigars,
When the gas-light shines full on your collar,
  It glitters with myriad stars,
That would n't look well at my wedding;
  They'd seem inappropriate there —
Nell does n't use diamond powder,
  She tells me it ruins the hair.

You've been out on Cozzens' piazza
  Too late, when the evenings were damp,
When the moon-beams were silvering Cro'nest,
  And the lights were all out in the camp.
You've rested on highly-oiled stair-ways
  Too often, when sweet eyes were bright,
And somebody's ball dress — Not Nellie's —
  Flowed round you in rivers of white.

There 's a reprobate looseness about you;
  Should I wear you to-night, I believe,
As I come with my bride from the altar,
  You 'd laugh in your wicked old sleeve,
When you felt there the tremulous pressure
  Of her hand, in its delicate glove,
That is telling me, shyly but proudly,
  Her trust is as deep as her love.

So, go to your grave in the wardrobe
  And furnish a feast for the moth,
Nell's glove shall betray its sweet secrets
  To younger, more innocent cloth.
' T is time to put on your successor —
  It 's made in a fashion that 's new;
Old coat, I 'm afraid it will never
  Set as easily on me as you.

DE LUNATICO

THE squadrons of the sun still hold
   The western hills; their armor lances,
Their crimson banners wide unfold,
   Low-levelled lie their golden lances.
The shadows lurk along the shore,
   Where, as our row-boat lightly passes,
The ripples, startled by my oar,
   Creep, murmuring, under drooping grasses.

Your eyes are downcast, for the light
   Is lingering round your face, forgetting
How late it is; for one last sight
   Of you the sun delays his setting.
One hand hangs idly from the boat,
   While round its white and swaying fingers —
Like half blown lilies gone afloat —
   The amorous water, toying, lingers.

I see you smile behind your book,
   Your sunny eyes concealing under
Their drooping lids, a fleeting look,
   That's partly fun, and partly wonder.
That I, a man of presence grave,
   Who fight for bread 'neath Themis' banner,
Should, all at once, begin to rave
   In this, I trust, Aldrichian manner.

You say our lake is — sad, but true! —
   The mill-pond of a Yankee village;
Its swelling shores devoted to
   The various forms of kitchen tillage;

That you 're no damsel bright and fair,
   And I no lover young and glowing,
Just an old, sober, married pair
   Who, after tea, have gone out rowing.

Ah, dear, when memories old and sweet
   Have fooled my senses thus, believe me,
Your dark eyes only helped the cheat,
   Your voice could never undeceive me.
I think it well that men, dear wife,
   Are sometimes with such madness smitten,
Else little joy would be in life,
   And little poetry be written.

HARRISON ROBERTSON
1850 –

APPROPRIATION

ONE day, one balmy "day of days,"
   I fortunately found her
Down in the sweet old garden's maze,
   Hid by its gloom around her.
She stood beneath the apple-tree,
   Against it idly leaning,
Gazing with eyes that did not see,
   Dreamy with subtle meaning.

She stood in snowy stuff bedight,
   Her lips a rose caressing,
Against the tree one nude and white
   Round arm her cheek was pressing.
Rich-favored tree — its boughs above
   In flaky banks were blowing,
Which, at the nearness of my love,
   In tender pink were glowing.

I paused, yet loth to spoil the scene,
   Content thus to adore her.
And then the shrubbery between
   I made my way before her.
A start — the slightest did it seem
   To me — such was my greeting.
Ah! had I been part of that *dream*
   Which scarcely yet was fleeting?

"I come into your life, my dear,
   As in your dream," I told her.
"I love you, and your place is here" —
   "Here" being next my shoulder.
Her place was there, her face was there
   Within her hands all hidden;
And on her rippling, sunny hair
   I pressed a kiss unchidden.

How sweet, among the apple-trees,
   The silent spell that bound us,
With naught but languid bloom and bees
   And mating birds around us.
"You have not said you love me yet,"
   At last I whispered to her.
She raised her eyes — ah! were they wet? —
   And as I nearer drew her,

Within their tender depths I read
   The answer I'd entreated;
No words of lips could have unsaid
   What those soft eyes repeated.
And then, with coy, maternal air,
   She smiled and touched my forehead,
"And, Jack, you must not comb your hair
   So high," she said — "it's horrid!"

THE STORY OF THE GATE

ACROSS the pathway, myrtle-fringed
   Under the maple, it was hinged —
 The little wooden gate:
'T was there within the quiet gloam,
When I had strolled with Nellie home,
   I used to pause and wait.

Before I said to her good-night,
Yet loath to leave the winsome sprite
   Within the garden's pale;
And there, the gate between us two,
We 'd linger, as all lovers do,
   And lean upon the rail.

And face to face, eyes close to eyes,
Hands meeting hands in feigned surprise
   After a stealthy quest,
So close I 'd bend, ere she 'd retreat,
That I 'd grow drunken from the sweet
   Carnations on her breast.

We 'd talk — in fitful style, I ween —
With many a meaning glance between
   The tender words and low;
We 'd whisper some dear sweet conceit,
Some idle gossip we 'd repeat;
   And then I 'd move to go.

"Good-night," I 'd say: "good-night — good-bye!"
"Good-night" — from her, with half a sigh —
   "Good-night!" "Good-night!" And then

And then I do not go, but stand,
Again lean on the railing, and
　　Begin it all again!

Ah! that was many a day ago —
That pleasant summer-time — although
　　The gate is standing yet;
A little cranky, it may be,
A little weather-worn — like me —
　　Who never can forget.

The happy — "End?" My cynic friend,
Pray save your sneers — there was no "end."
　　Watch yonder chubby thing! —
That is our youngest — hers and mine ·
See how he climbs, his legs to twine
　　About the gate and swing.

EUGENE FIELD
1850 – 1895

[From "*A Little Book of Western Verse.*" Copyright, 1889, by *Eugene Field*]

LONG AGO

I ONCE knew all the birds that came
   And nested in our orchard trees;
For every flower I had a name —
   My friends were woodchucks, toads and bees
I knew where thrived in yonder glen
   What plants would sooth a stone-bruised toe —
Oh, I was very learned then;
   But that was very long ago!

I knew the spot upon the hill
   Where checkerberries could be found,
I knew the rushes near the mill
   Where pickerel lay that weighed a pound!
I knew the wood, — the very tree
   Where lived the poaching, saucy crow,
And all the woods and crows knew me —
   But that was very long ago.

And pining for the joys of youth,
   I tread the old familiar spot
Only to learn this solemn truth:
   I have forgotten, am forgot.

Yet here 's this youngster at my knee
  Knows all the things I used to know;
To think I once was wise as he —
  But that was very long ago.

I know it 's folly to complain
  Of whatsoe'er the Fates decree;
Yet were not wishes all in vain,
  I tell you what my wish should be:
I 'd wish to be a boy again,
  Back with the friends I used to know;
  For I was, oh! so happy then —
But that was very long ago!

THIRTY-NINE

O HAPLESS day! O wretched day!
   I hoped you'd pass me by —
Alas, the years have sneaked away
   And all is changed but I!
Had I the power, I would remand
   You to a gloom condign,
But here you've crept upon me and
   I — I am thirty-nine!

Now, were I thirty-five, I could
   Assume a flippant guise;
Or, were I forty years, I should
   Undoubtedly look wise;
For forty years are said to bring
   Sedateness superfine;
But thirty-nine don't mean a thing —
   A bas with thirty-nine!

You healthy, hulking girls and boys, —
   What makes you grow so fast?
Oh, I'll survive your lusty noise —
   I'm tough and bound to last!
No, no — I'm old and withered too —
   I feel my powers decline,
(Yet none believes this can be true
   Of one at thirty-nine.)

And you, dear girl with velvet eyes
   I wonder what you mean
Through all our keen anxieties
   By keeping sweet sixteen.

With your dear love to warm my heart,
  Wretch were I to repine;
I was but jesting at the start —
  I 'm glad I 'm thirty-nine!

So, little children, roar and race
  As blithely as you can,
And, sweetheart, let your tender grace
  Exalt the Day and Man;
For then these factors (I 'll engage)
  All subtly shall combine
To make both juvenile and sage
  The one who 's thirty-nine!

Yes, after all, I 'm free to say
  I would much rather be
Standing as I do stand to-day,
  'Twixt devil and deep sea;
For though my face be dark with care
  Or with a grimace shine,
Each haply falls unto my share,
  For I am thirty-nine!

'T is passing meet to make good cheer
  And lord it like a king,
Since only once we catch the year
  That does n't mean a thing.
O happy day! O gracious day!
  I pledge thee in this wine —
Come, let us journey on our way
  A year, good Thirty-Nine!

APPLE–PIE AND CHEESE

FULL many a sinful notion
    Conceived of foreign powers
Has come across the ocean
    To harm this land of ours;
And heresies called fashions
    Have modesty effaced,
And baleful, morbid passions
    Corrupt our native taste.
O tempora! O mores!
    What profanations these
That seek to dim the glories
    Of apple-pie and cheese!

I'm glad my education
    Enables me to stand
Against the vile temptation
    Held out on every hand.
Eschewing all the tittles
    With vanity replete,
I'm loyal to the victuals
    Our grandsires used to eat!
I'm glad I've got three willing boys
    To hang around and tease
Their mother for the filling joys
    Of apple-pie and cheese!

Your flavored creams and ices
    And your dainty angel-food
Are mighty fine devices
    To regale the dainty dude;

Your terrapin and oysters,
　　With wine to wash 'em down,
Are just the thing for roisters
　　When painting of the town;
No flippant, sugared notion
　　Shall *my* appetite appease,
Or bate my soul's devotion
　　To apple-pie and cheese!

The pie my Julia makes me
　　(God bless her Yankee ways!)
On memory's pinions takes me
　　To dear Green Mountain days;
And seems like I saw Mother
　　Lean on the window-sill,
A-handin' me and brother
　　What she knows 'll keep us still;
And these feelings are so grateful,
　　Says I, "Julia, if you please,
I 'll take another plateful
　　Of that apple-pie and cheese!"

And cheese! No alien it, sir,
　　That 's brought across the sea, —
No Dutch antique, nor Switzer,
　　Nor glutinous de Brie;
There 's nothing I abhor so
　　As mawmets of this ilk —
Give *me* the harmless morceau
　　That 's made of true-blue milk!
No matter what conditions
　　Dyspeptic come to feaze,
The best of all physicians
　　Is apple-pie and cheese!

Though ribalds may decry 'em,
　　For these twin boons we stand,
Partaking thrice per diem
　　Of their fulness out of hand;

No enervating fashion
  Shall cheat us of our right
To gratify our passion
  With a mouthful at a bite!
We'll cut it square or bias,
  Or any way we please,
And faith shall justify us
  When we carve our pie and cheese!

De gustibus, 't is stated,
  Non disputandum est.
Which meaneth, when translated,
  That all is for the best.
So let the foolish choose 'em
  The vapid sweets of sin,
I will not disabuse 'em
  Of the heresy they're in;
But I, when I undress me
  Each night, upon my knees
Will ask the Lord to bless me
  With apple-pie and cheese!

EUGENE FIELD

OLD TIMES, OLD FRIENDS, OLD LOVE [1]

THERE are no days like the good old days, —
    The days when we were youthful!
When humankind were pure of mind,
    And speech and deeds were truthful;
Before a love for sordid gold
    Became man's ruling passion,
And before each dame and maid became
    Slave to the tyrant fashion!

There are no girls like the good old girls, —
    Against the world I'd stake 'em!
As buxom and smart and clean of heart
    As the Lord knew how to make 'em!
They were rich in spirit and common-sense,
    And piety all supportin';
They could bake and brew, and had taught school, too,
    And they made such likely courtin'!

There are no boys like the good old boys, —
    When *we* were boys together!
When the grass was sweet to the brown bare feet
    That dimpled the laughing heather;
When the pewee sung to the summer dawn
    Of the bee in the billowy clover,
Or down by the mill the whip-poor-will
    Echoed his night song over.

[1] From "Second Book of Verse." Copyright, 1892, by Julia Sutherland Field.

There is no love like the good old love, —
　　The love that mother gave us!
We are old, old men, yet we pine again
　　For that precious grace, — God save us!
So we dream and dream of the good old times,
　　And our hearts grow tenderer, fonder,
As those dear old dreams bring soothing gleams
　　Of heaven away off yonder.

IRWIN RUSSELL
1853–1879

COSMOS

WHAT to me are all your treasures?
    Have I need of purchased pleasures,
      Crœsus, such as thine?
Come, I'll have thee make confession
Thou hast naught in thy possession,
      And the world is mine.

I have all that thou hadst never;
Though I'm old, I'm young forever,
      And happy I, at ease;
All I wish I can create it;
Wing my soul, and elevate it
      Where and when I please.

Of my secret make but trial:
Seest thou this little vial?
      Dost thou not, then, think
Magic power to it pertaining,
All the world itself containing,
      Though it holds but — INK?

HENRY CUYLER BUNNER
1855 – 1896

[*From " The Poems of H. C. Bunner."* Copyright, *1884, 1892, 1896, 1899, by Charles Scribner's Sons*]

THE WAY TO ARCADY

OH, what's the way to Arcady,
　To Arcady, to Arcady;
Oh, what's the way to Arcady,
　Where all the leaves are merry?

Oh, what's the way to Arcady?
The spring is rustling in the tree, —
The tree the wind is blowing through,
　It sets the blossoms flickering white.
I knew not skies could burn so blue
　Nor any breezes blow so light.
They blow an old-time way for me,
Across the world to Arcady.

Oh, what's the way to Arcady?
Sir Poet, with the rusty coat,
Quit mocking of the song-bird's note.
How have you heart for any tune,
You with the wayworn russet shoon?
Your scrip, a-swinging by your side,
Gapes with a gaunt mouth hungry-wide.
I'll brim it well with pieces red,
If you will tell the way to tread.

Oh, I am bound for Arcady,
And if you but keep pace with me
You tread the way to Arcady.

And where away lies Arcady,
And how long yet may the journey be?

Ah, that (quoth he) *I do not know:*
Across the clover and the snow —
Across the frost, across the flowers —
Through summer seconds and winter hours,
I've trod the way my whole life long,
   And know not now where it may be;
My guide is but the stir to song,
That tells me I cannot go wrong,
   Or clear or dark the pathway be
   Upon the road to Arcady.

But how shall I do who cannot sing?
   I was wont to sing, once on a time, —
There is never an echo now to ring
   Remembrance back to the trick of rhyme.

'Tis strange you cannot sing (quoth he), —
The folk all sing in Arcady.

But how may he find Arcady
Who hath nor youth nor melody?

What, know you not, old man (quoth he), —
   Your hair is white, your face is wise, —
   That Love must kiss that Mortal's eyes
Who hopes to see fair Arcady?
No gold can buy you entrance there;
But beggared Love may go all bare —
No wisdom won with weariness;
But Love goes in with Folly's dress —
No fame that wit could ever win;
But only Love may lead Love in
   To Arcady, to Arcady.

Ah, woe is me, through all my days
  Wisdom and wealth I both have got,
And fame and name, and great men's praise;
  But Love, ah Love! I have it not.
There was a time, when life was new —
  But far away, and half forgot —
I only know her eyes were blue;
  But Love — I fear I knew it not.
We did not wed, for lack of gold,
And she is dead, and I am old.
All things have come since then to me,
Save Love, ah Love! and Arcady.

Ah, then I fear we part (quoth he), —
My way's for Love and Arcady.

But you, you fare alone, like me;
  The gray is likewise in your hair.
What love have you to lead you there,
  To Arcady, to Arcady?

Ah, no, not lonely do I fare;
  My true companion's Memory.
With Love he fills the Spring-time air;
  With Love he clothes the Winter tree.
Oh, past this poor horizon's bound
  My song goes straight to one who stands, —
Her face all gladdening at the sound, —
  To lead me to the Spring-green lands,
To wander with enlacing hands.
The songs within my breast that stir
Are all of her, are all of her.
My maid is dead long years (quoth he), —
She waits for me in Arcady.

Oh, yon's the way to Arcady,
  To Arcady, to Arcady;
Oh, yon's the way to Arcady,
  Where all the leaves are merry.

CANDOR

OCTOBER — A WOOD

"I KNOW what you 're going to say," she said,
   And she stood up, looking uncommonly tall:
"You are going to speak of the hectic fall,
And say you 're sorry the summer 's dead,
   And no other summer was like it, you know,
   And can I imagine what made it so.
Now are n't you, honestly?" "Yes," I said.

" I know what you 're going to say," she said:
   " You are going to ask if I forget
That day in June when the woods were wet,
And you carried me " — here she drooped her head —
   "Over the creek; you are going to say,
   Do I remember that horrid day.
Now are n't you, honestly?" "Yes," I said.

"I know what you 're going to say," she said:
   "You are going to say that since that time
You have rather tended to run to rhyme,
And " — her clear glance fell, and her cheek grew red —
   " And have I noticed your tone was queer.
   Why, *everybody* has seen it here!
Now are n't you, honestly?" "Yes," I said.

"I know what *you* 're going to say," I said:
   " You 're going to say you 've been much annoyed;
And I 'm short of tact — you will say, 'devoid' —
And I 'm clumsy and awkward; and call me Ted;
   And I bear abuse like a dear old lamb;
   And you 'll have me, anyway, just as I am.
Now are n't you, honestly?" "Ye-es," she said.

"ONE, TWO, THREE!"

IT was an old, old, old, old lady,
   And a boy who was half-past three;
And the way that they played together
   Was beautiful to see.

She could n't go running and jumping,
   And the boy, no more could he.
For he was a thin little fellow,
   With a thin, little, twisted knee.

They sat in the yellow sunlight,
   Out under the maple-tree;
And the game that they played I 'll tell you,
   Just as it was told to me.

It was Hide-and-Go-Seek they were playing,
   Though you 'd never have known it to be —
With an old, old, old, old lady,
   And a boy with a twisted knee.

The boy would bend his face down
   On his one little sound right knee,
And he 'd guess where she was hiding,
   In guesses One, Two, Three!

"You are in the china-closet!"
   He would cry, and laugh with glee —
It was n't the china-closet;
   But he still had Two and Three.

"You are up in Papa's big bedroom,
   In the chest with the queer old key!"
And she said: "You are *warm* and *warmer;*
   But you 're not quite right," said she.

"It can't be the little cupboard
　　Where Mamma's things used to be —
So it must be the clothes-press, Gran'ma!"
　　And he found her, with his Three.

Then she covered her face with her fingers,
　　That were wrinkled and white and wee,
And she guessed where the boy was hiding,
　　With a One and a Two and a Three.

And they never had stirred from their places,
　　Right under the maple-tree —
This old, old, old, old lady,
　　And the boy with the lame little knee —
This dear, dear, dear old lady,
　　And the boy who was half-past three.

THE CHAPERON

Take my chaperon to the play —
  She thinks she's taking me —
And the gilded youth who owns the box,
  A proud young man is he.
But how would his young heart be hurt
  If he could only know
    That not for his sweet sake I go,
    Nor yet to see the trifling show;
But to see my chaperon flirt.

Her eyes beneath her snowy hair
  They sparkle young as mine;
There's scarce a wrinkle in her hand
  So delicate and fine.
And when my chaperon is seen,
  They come from everywhere —
    The dear old boys with silvery hair,
    With old-time grace and old-time air,
To greet their old-time queen.

They bow as my young Midas here
  Will never learn to bow
(The dancing-masters do not teach
  That gracious reverence now);
With voices quavering just a bit,
  They play their old parts through,
    They talk of folk who used to woo,
    Of hearts that broke in 'fifty-two —
Now none the worse for it.

And as those aged crickets chirp
   I watch my chaperon's face,
And see the dear old features take
   A new and tender grace —
And in her happy eyes I see
   Her youth awakening bright,
   With all its hope, desire, delight —
   Ah, me! I wish that I were quite
As young — as young as she!

FORFEITS

THEY sent him round the circle fair,
  To bow before the prettiest there.
I'm bound to say the choice he made
A creditable taste displayed;
Although — I can't say what it meant —
The little maid looked ill-content.

His task was then anew begun —
To kneel before the wittiest one.
Once more that little maid sought he,
And went him down upon his knee.
She bent her eyes upon the floor —
I think she thought the game a bore.

He circled then — his sweet behest
To kiss the one he loved the best.
For all she frowned, for all she chid,
He kissed that little maid, he did.
And then — though why I can't decide —
The little maid looked satisfied.

CHARLES HENRY LÜDERS

1858 – 1891

MY MAIDEN AUNT

[*From " The Dead Nymph and Other Poems." Copyright, 1891,
by Charles Scribner's Sons*]

DEAR withered cheek — you know the hue,
　Old parchment; something of a shrew,
She has not — between me and you —
　　Lived much " in clover."
Yet seldom is she heard to sigh;
And when she smiles, from either eye
The radiating wrinkles fly
　　Her face all over.

Time, laying by his scythe, I trow,
Has guided his relentless plow
Across the pallor of a brow
　　Once far from homely.
And russet curls, that once she tossed
Coquettishly, are crisped with frost,
But have not altogether lost
　　Their hue so comely.

I've heard — from whom I can't aver —
That fate has been unkind to her;
Old letters laid in lavender
　　Reveal a lover.

But these are dated long ago,
And years have yellowed o'er their snow,
Since she, with tell-tale cheeks aglow,
   First read them over.

In escapades of day and night,
When she has risen in her might,
I've found that though her foot is light
   Her hand is heavy.
Yet, though at times she loves to pour
The vials of her anger o'er
My head, she keeps a warm spot for
   Her graceless "nevvy."

How oft the teasing gibe I've checked
Upon my tongue, to recollect
That she, so long denied respect,
   Does now command some.
I would not dare to even *grin*
At her, my wealthy next-of-kin,
Lest, some day, I might *not* come in
   For something handsome.

RICHARD HOVEY
1864 – 1900

A TOAST

HERE'S a health to thee, Roberts,
    And here's a health to me;
And here's to all the pretty girls
    From Denver to the sea!

Here's to mine and here's to thine!
    Now's the time to clink it!
Here's a flagon of old wine,
    And here we are to drink it.

Wine that maketh glad the heart
    Of the bully boy!
Here's the toast that we love most,
    "Love and song and joy!"

Song that is the flower of love,
    And joy that is the fruit!
Here's the love of woman, lad,
    And here's our love to boot!

You and I are far too wise
    Not to fill our glasses.
Here's to me and here's to thee,
    And here's to all the lasses!

THE LOVE OF A BOY — TO-DAY

HEIGH-HO! my thoughts are far away;
  For wine or books I have no care;
I like to think upon the way
She has of looking very fair.
    Oh, work is nought, and play is nought,
    And all the livelong day is nought;
    There's nothing much I care to learn
    But what her lovely lips have taught.

The campus cannot tempt me out,
The classics cannot keep me in;
The only place I care about
Is where perchance she may have been.
    Oh, work is nought, and play is nought,
    And all the livelong day is nought;
    There's nothing much I care to find
    Except the way she would be sought.

The train across the valley screams,
And like a hawk sweeps out of sight;
It bears me to her in my dreams
By day and night, by day and night.
    Oh, work is nought, and play is nought,
    And all the livelong day is nought;
    There's nothing much I care to be,
    If I be only in her thought.

ANNE REEVE ALDRICH
1866 – 1892

[*From " Songs About Life, Love and Death."* Copyright, *1892, by Charles Scribner's Sons*]

SOUVENIRS

Mais où sont les neiges d'antan?

WHERE is the glove that I gave to him,
  Perfumed and warm from my arm that night?
And where is the rose that another stole
When the land was flooded with June moonlight,
And the satin slipper I wore? — Alack,
  Some one had that — it was wrong, I fear.
Where are those souvenirs to-day?
  But where are the snows of yester-year?

The glove was burned at his next love's prayer,
And the rose was lost in the mire of the street;
And the satin slipper he tossed away,
For his jealous bride had not fairy feet.
Give what you will, but know, mesdames,
  For a day alone are your favors dear.
Be sure for the next fair woman's sake
  They will go — like the snows of yester-year.

FANNY

A SOUTHERN BLOSSOM

COME and see her as she stands,
  Crimson roses in her hands;
    And her eyes
Are as dark as Southern night,
Yet than Southern dawn more bright,
And a soft, alluring light
    In them lies.

None deny if she beseech
  With that pretty, liquid speech
    Of the South.
All her consonants are slurred,
And the vowels are preferred;
There's a poem in each word
    From that mouth.

Even Cupid is her slave;
Of his arrows, half he gave
    Her one day
In a merry, playful hour.
Dowered with these and beauty's dower,
Strong indeed her magic power,
    So they say.

Venus, not to be outdone
By her generous little son,
    Shaped the mouth
Very like to Cupid's bow.
Lack-a-day! Our North can show
No such lovely flowers as grow
    In the South!